NOTHING
Matters

"*Heart containing nothing*" cover artwork by Gini Baillie.
Gini had a glioblastoma of the brain with short-term
memory loss and often used drawings to communicate.
She began with brown to make "a lamb" then added black
and yellow and said it was "nothing." She followed this with
a "red heart"—all in watercolor inkpencil with partial wash.

Laurie —
May the Lord direct your steps
as you find your significance
only in Him   Gene Baillie
Ps 73:25 (21-28) Phil 2:3-4

When you first read the two words *Nothing Matters*, you default to the usual cultural meaning of the word *nothing*, but if you think a moment, there is a noun and a verb. Nouns are something, and thus the nothing is really something that matters! Years ago, I was intrigued by the casual way we use the word *nothing* in our culture. Thus began my thinking about nothing then writing about nothing, all the time truly realizing that nothing has to be something. We simply use the word when we do not know or understand the *real something* we are conscious of quite deep within. Look at the world around us and see the mathematical zero taught to us as nil, naught—it is really an entity that is defined and has rules, and we can actually have something that is less than zero. We also see that high tide is a real something, that instant of seeming "no thing" when the tide is neither coming in nor going out—nevertheless, a real entity that we assign a name. *Nothing* is seen throughout the Scriptures. The Bible teaches us that we come into the world "with nothing" and will certainly "take nothing" as we leave this world. My desire is to challenge you to think about your life and its true purpose, so that you do not waste your nothing. You see, *nothing* truly does matter!

When we cry out to God and nothing seems to change, nothing is really changing! We may think God is doing nothing in response to our prayers, but be assured He is not wasting this "nothing"! And deep down we know that He truly is doing something, just not acting in the way we desire or even see. What appears to be undesirable to us for the moment or for a lifetime is still God's answer and response to our prayer, even if it appears to not be anything. God works through even the worst affliction to accomplish far more than we can even imagine at the moment, even to coming generations.

~

Nothing Matters *is a* different *sort of book, for sure—but one that will speak to many as through it they are provoked to consider what God is doing in the 'nothing' moments of their lives. Oh, that we might all 'be still' and know that He is God.*

— Scott Anderson, Executive Director
Desiring God Ministries

"Nothing will ever be the same." After you read this book, you will see why these carefully chosen words define the effect and message of this book on me, and now you! . . . I will never think of nothing the same way again!

— Dr. Dale Treash, pediatrician, Anderson, SC

Much of the fast pace of life clouds what really matters and sidetracks our efforts to focus on the eternal. We make much of everything instead of making much of nothing.

— Karen Rigsby, Director of Family Ministry
Fellowship Greenville, Greenville, SC

~

To order additional copies of this book or
to obtain in e-book format, go to
www.ReadNothingMatters.com
or www.ReadGoodBooks.org

Dr. Gene Baillie

NOTHING
Matters

Finding Significance

The quoted ideas expressed in this book (but not Scripture verses) are not, in all cases, exact quotations, as some have been edited for clarity and brevity. In all cases, the author has attempted to maintain the speaker's original intent. In some cases, quoted material for this book was obtained from secondary sources, primarily print media. While every effort was made to ensure the accuracy of these sources, the accuracy cannot be guaranteed.

Unless noted otherwise, Scripture quotations are from the Holy Bible, English Standard Version (ESV), which is adapted from the Revised Standard Version of the Bible, copyright Division of Christian Education of the National Council of the Churches of Christ in the U.S.A. All rights reserved.

Scripture quotations marked KJV are from the Holy Bible, King James Version; NKJV, the Holy Bible, New King James Version, copyright © 1982 by Thomas Nelson, Inc., used by permission; HCSB, the Holman Christian Standard Bible,™ copyright © 1999, 2000, 2001 by Holman Bible Publishers, used by permission; NIV, the Holy Bible, New International Version,® copyright © 1973, 1978, 1984 International Bible Society, used by permission of Zondervan, all rights reserved; NASB, the New American Standard Bible,® copyright © 1960, 1962, 1963, 1968, 1971, 1972, 1973, 1975, 1977, 1995 by the Lockman Foundation, used by permission; NRSV, New Revised Standard Version Bible, copyright 1989, Division of Christian Education of the National Council of the Churches of Christ in the United States of America, used by permission, all rights reserved.

Cover by Diana Lawrence
Page layout and e-book by Lisa Parnell

ISBN 978-0-9964972-0-6

Printed in United States of America

22 21 20 19 18 17 16 15   1 2 3 4 5

Contents

Foreword

I read this book! In the midst of a very hectic few months with a son graduating from college, as well as his moving, getting married, and having knee surgery, I read this book! My read-through was perfectly timed to coincide with the hectic pace of life at the time. I knew from the first few pages when I read, "We must remember not to waste the pauses and stillness—the times of doing nothing together. . . . Nothing is simple. . . . Everything is complicated. . . . Nothing is significant," that God had something (not nothing) in mind for me to encounter in the pages of the book.

The book did a great job of zooming in on the idea of "nothing" and zooming out to where "nothing" is encountered in the world, the Bible, and in my life. The idea that my nothing that I came into the world with, my soul, is at the very core of my life on this earth was an awakening thought. And, although that idea is overwhelming, when I depend on His work to make something out of my nothing, He does not leave me useless and my soul can be something of value. The book beautifully reminded me that when God gives me His love He not only promises me life eternal but takes my nothing and makes something useful for Him. He redeems everything for His purposes and glory.

As my boys are leaving home and physically not near me on a daily basis, it was encouraging to be reminded, "We simply cannot fully understand what the other person [my sons] is going through, but if we are *in tune*, we can *feel* the 'vibes' and can *hear* the process [of connecting] resounding in our head." This section of the book was balm to my soul—I can stay connected to my boys in many ways, but I especially need to hear their hearts.

Another big reminder for me was that much of the fast pace of life clouds what really matters and sidetracks my efforts to focus on the eternal. I make much of everything instead of making much of nothing. I allow the demands of the world to bog me down. While overall I would say I seek God's direction during my earthly life, the book reminded me that on a moment-by-moment basis I need to seek God's direction. I've allowed my perspective to be clouded with everything. The book reminded me "Only God is able to make us see exactly who we are and make us feel truly confident at the same time." He shows me that I am nothing on my own, but He, Christ, is everything and without Him I have no value. My perspective had gotten a little off—thanks for the course correction.

— Karen Rigsby
Director of Family Ministry
Fellowship Greenville
Greenville, SC

Acknowledgments

I want to thank and praise God for giving me the ability and clarity to write the important truths contained in this book. He created the universe and all that is in it, is light for the path we walk, adopted us into His family for all eternity, and gave us His Word with promises and provision for our daily needs. During our time as aliens and strangers on this earth, we have been the recipient of God's grace and direction for each step we take. While we follow His leading, and even know He is holding our hand, we gratefully acknowledge that He has given us all things—our soul and body, life and breath, worldly abilities, and provision for our needs, as well as saving faith to acknowledge Him as Savior, Lord, and Treasure. As we give Him glory and honor, may we never lose sight of knowing that what He has begun in us He will complete according to His plan and in His perfect timing.

Thanks also to Anna Dunlap Renfro, a friend who was paid to think and write about *nothing*! She spent many hours at the computer, went through many critiques, and took my notes and helped organize the first draft of this book.

A special thanks to Carl Robbins and Scott Anderson who not only reviewed the manuscript and suggested clarifications but also guided and reviewed my theological thinking. I thank Dale Treash, Chase Marshburn, John Boyte, and Elsie Newell for reviewing, editing, and providing helpful comments as well as encouragement. And, finally, I thank Lisa Parnell, who helped with copyediting and layout, and Diana Lawrence, who helped with the cover design using Gini's artwork.

A Message
to Readers

This book is a testimony, a reprimand, and a call for change, a sort of three in one. However, it is not about the word *nothing* as we usually consider it. It is about opening our eyes to understanding human life and whether it has significance. Only when our heart understands its nothingness can we truly embrace our human value and purpose. Only when we see that we are but a clay pot (2 Corinthians 4:7), useless unless filled, will we ever beg for water (Jeremiah 2:13).

Before we delve too deeply into "nothingness," I first want to state that the aim of this book is to glorify God. It is not just a collection of ideas that provides pleasantries to our minds. No, these ideas have a message to deliver.

A deadly brain tumor has a way of getting one's attention, making both its victim and those around them reevaluate life and death. When my wife of more than 51 years was diagnosed with a glioblastoma of her right frontal brain and given six months to two years to live, our lives changed. Questions constantly surfaced and confronted us—the purpose of suffering, the brevity of life, the unexpected nature and certainty of death, and the acute awareness of one's time left to make a difference in this world. Is life just nothing (in the sense of not anything), or is life something preparing us for our future? When a strong, healthy person rapidly declines into a nearly helpless state, those who love her suffer alongside her. Many people have wondered at the peace and (even) joy we both had in this extremely difficult season of life. I, too, marveled many times. Still, I can confidently say that my hope is the fruit of believing in a Sovereign God who has a perfect plan for our days, who uses every part of our lives for His eternal purposes, and who does not leave anything, not even lethal cancer, wasted. And I can assure you that life is not just nothing!

When you picked up this book, you may have been wondering what in the world it was about. Is this old retired guy only going to discuss what it's like to finally be able to sit around with little to do? Is it an older man's reprimand to young people who seem to be living their lives with no direction and making "nothing" of themselves? Or, maybe he is asking something of a generation who has lost the art of communication and thinking, who are lazily abusing the word *nothing*.

The genesis for this book came from notes jotted down long before the wife of my life had her tumor, but now they have been heated in the furnace of afflictions so that some dross has been removed. My prayer is that God has directed these words to you specifically so you will understand the part of you that is *nothing* and know exactly how important that nothing is to your life on earth. I have written this book to convince you that nothing is really something!

I have used Scripture, the world around us, Bible study, reflections at conferences, books, and conversations. I almost never wrote down the person or source of the information. While the information I have included may be anonymous to you and me, it is not anonymous to God. He laid it before me clearly using many means. After all, His truth is immutable. It does not change with passing decades or centuries or traveling from person to person.

The first purpose of this book is to present the concepts and understanding of the term *nothing* from an approach that challenges our usual thinking (or lack thereof). We use the word *nothing* flippantly, but how does God use it? How does the Creator use nothing in nature and in Scripture, and how does He use nothing in us? What does the Bible mean when it says, "For we brought nothing into this world, and it is certain we can carry nothing out" (1 Timothy 6:7 NKJV)?

The second purpose of this book is to catalyze in you a desire to live life not wasted, no matter the kind of moment in life you find yourself. My hope is that you will be encouraged and inspired toward more purposeful living, knowing that in Christ your life has a purpose. In every season, He wants your good, that you might live each moment for His glory, knowing that His plan for your particular life is purposeful in its entirety.

Are you someone who seeks reassurance that your life has meaning and can be one of great purpose? Read on. Come into these pages with an open mind, ready to be challenged. Ready to think. Ready to be changed.

Truly, we came into this world with nothing—and with God's help, let us desire to not waste that nothing. Get ready to see *nothing* as you never have before!

— E Eugene Baillie, MD, 2015

NOTHING
Matters

Men have a great deal of pleasure in human knowledge, in studies of natural things; but this is nothing to that joy which arises from divine light shining into the soul. This spiritual light is the dawning of the light of glory in the heart. There is nothing so powerful as this to support persons in affliction, and to give the mind peace and brightness in this stormy and dark world. This knowledge will wean from the world, and raise the inclination to heavenly things. It will turn the heart to God as the fountain of good, and to choose him for the only portion. This light, and this only, will bring the soul to a saving close with Christ. It conforms the heart to the gospel, mortifies its enmity and opposition against the scheme of salvation therein revealed: it causes the heart to embrace the joyful tidings, and entirely to adhere to, and acquiesce in the revelation of Christ as our Savior.

The beauty of the world consists wholly of sweet mutual consents, either within itself, or with the Supreme Being.

Almost all men, and those that seem to be very miserable, love life, because they cannot bear to lose sight of such a beautiful and lovely world. The ideas, that every moment whilst we live have a beauty that we take not distinct notice of, brings a pleasure that, when we come to the trial, we had rather live in much pain and misery than lose.

— Jonathan Edwards,
"The Beauty of the World," 1725

If nothing is truly the absence of everything, how can it still be a noun? If it is the nonexistence of all things, why do we still talk about it? Why and how can nothing still exist as a crucial part of our language and lives if it is really not anything?

1. Nothing Has Meaning

What are you thinking about? Nothing. What are you doing? Nothing. What do we have left in our bank account? Nothing. What do I have to offer? Nothing. What do I mean to this world? Nothing. What good could come of this? Nothing. What did I do wrong? Nothing. What can I do to make it up to you? Nothing.

These are all important questions. The answers could be read as empty, hopeless, negative, pessimistic, and discouraging, even disconnected. And apart from Christ, I agree that we truly can do nothing. We are nothing. We have nothing to offer. And besides, we can do nothing to make up for our failures.

But the beauty of the gospel is that God redeems everything. He works all things for good. He even redeems our nothing. In God's economy, when we have nothing to offer, that is something. When we have done nothing, actually that is something. When it seems that nothing good can come from a circumstance, God is making something good, every time.

Nothing truly does matter, a lot! I would like you to join me on a journey through nothingness—areas the world considers to be nothing. I would like to convince you that God is in all of those times of apparent emptiness, waiting, loneliness, helplessness, boredom.

We often hear the following quotes. I have made a comment or explanatory statement after several of them.

"I'm sure it is nothing." Typical of most that follow, this has a double meaning.

"Do you mean I'm doing this for nothing?" Yes you are!

"You are trying to make something out of nothing."

"I'm good. I have nothing to hide."

"I can do nothing."

"Nothing can save me."

"Nothing is wrong with me."

"Nothing is going on." Read that carefully! First, there is *nothing*; second, it is *going*.

"I see nothing good in this."

"Nothing important." Must be something that is considered important!

"I am so busy doing *nothing* that the idea of doing *anything*—which, as you know, always leads to *something*—cuts into the nothing and then forces me to have to drop *everything*." This is from *Seinfeld*, which consisted of 172 episodes of . . . (you guessed it) nothing.

"You are nothing to me."

My computer just gave me a click-point choice: "Do nothing."

"That is nothing to worry about."

"Nothing will ever separate us." Think through this one!

"You bring nothing to the table."

"Nothing is idle."

A quote from *Alice's Adventures in Wonderland*: "What do you know about this business?" "Nothing." "Nothing *whatever*?" "Nothing whatever." "That's very important."

"That is about as close to nothing as you can get."

"Nothing jumps out from the page at me!" If nothing is absolutely not anything, then it cannot be a noun and cannot jump.

"I get nothing out of that."

"I'll tell you one thing: I have nothing to give!"

"Nothing is simple."

"I have nothing."

"I am nothing."

"Nothing I need."

And in the song "Something Good" from *The Sound of Music*, there is a mention of where nothing comes from, which you might find interesting to look up. I choose not to pay a fee to print just two lines.

A Note about Nothing

As a child, I can remember my mom saying there was nothing between my ears. And, in a real sense, she was right. One could say I've had nothing between my ears for my whole life! Thoughts about the concept of the significance of nothing in language, nature, and Scripture have been bouncing around in my brain for many years, but those thoughts never seemed to sit still long enough to solidify. They came from a myriad of readings, circumstances, statements, and conversations that seemed random, and yet I knew they were providentially connected because I believe that our sovereign God is in charge of every detail of His universe.

One of these seemingly random interactions was with my wife, Gini. She had already been diagnosed with the glioblastoma multiforme—the worst and most deadly cancer that starts in the brain. The Lord was gracious to allow a near-complete removal of the tumor and success with chemo and radiation treatments. After a very deep valley, the wife of my life again emerged from weakness and mental fog enough to function quite well with help. One discovery we made was that she could still recall large passages of Scripture she had memorized. They were her comfort on difficult days.

One day I checked on her while she was resting, and she said, "If you aren't too busy and have nothing better to do, can you hold my hand?" After I cried a bucket of tears, I sat holding her hand as I have done so many times during our more than fifty years of marriage. As I sat quietly "doing nothing" with her, I realized her comment about *nothing* was profound. By only holding her hand, I was really doing almost nothing, but the nothing I was doing was everything she wanted and needed at the time. I had this over-whelming feeling of love, and I knew she sensed it

> *Be still, and know that I am God.*
> — Psalm 46:10 NKJV

as well—without a word! I was struck with the thought that we must remember not to waste the pauses and stillness—the times of doing nothing together (which is really something!)—anymore than the times of the hectic pace, passion, and silliness of our loving one another. Both concepts are valuable, and together they make the whole of life. Sometimes doing nothing is what makes those fuller times so special.

As I get older and closer to the end of my time on this earth, the pauses and stillness parts of my life seem to be far more important concepts. And I hope you noticed all the things I just wrote about besides the *no-thing*. There were the some-things, the every-things, and all-things!

The reminder from my wife was but one of a million thoughts my brain contrived. Increasingly in the past couple of years, I have continued to make notes—ideas and sentences penned here and there—then put them aside for an occasional revisit. Dreams of compiling them into a book seemed too lofty to tackle. But, the Holy Spirit pressed me to share my own observations and understanding of nothingness, and the book idea surfaced again one day when I read a note that I had written in 1 Corinthians during my annual Bible read-through years ago. In the note, I connected 1 Corinthians 1:28 and 2:2 by circling a word found in both verses and drawing a line between them. The verses that Paul penned read:

> God chose what is low and despised in the world, even things that are not, to bring to nothing things that are. (1 Corinthians 1:28)

and

> For I decided to know nothing among you except Jesus Christ and Him crucified. (1 Corinthians 2:2)

The unifying word I had circled was *nothing*. Across the line bridging the two words was my written phrase, "Don't waste your nothing." (I realized that I wrote the note after reading John Piper's book *Don't Waste Your Life*.) I decided to re-read and seriously study the first two chapters of 1 Corinthians, which then caused all the puzzle pieces in my head to form a more complete picture.

In these first two chapters of 1 Corinthians, we are specifically told to consider our calling, yet God says in the two verses cited above that He wants it brought to nothing so that we have no boast outside of Him.

In addition the Lord exemplifies through Paul the importance of knowing nothing (in the sense of not anything) except Jesus Christ and Him crucified. My intrigue was rekindled by the use of the term *nothing* as well as words like "things that are not," "something," "anything," and "things that are." Finally, the concept clicked. Our lives, in and of themselves, are nothing. Nothing! Although this instance of the word *nothing* seemed to imply nothing at all or not anything at all, it could not be the absolute absence of all things. So, nothing has to be something!

Thus, a note written to myself in my Bible about *nothing* became a catalyst for my study and reflection. Though I am a layman and not a theologian, I discovered that the word *nothing* appears more than 250 times in the Bible (not always the same Hebrew or Greek word), and there are many other closely related terms and words. To me, nothing seemed to be multifaceted, useful for further understanding and application. Nothing even shows up in commands to use our nothingness for the glory of God and not for ourselves. Our lives—our nothing—should not be wasted. I now want to channel your thoughts that hopefully ask you to stop, ponder truth, think, and then live with purpose.

A Definition of Nothing

"Nothing is simple." Think about that sentence for a minute. At first thought, our minds immediately comprehend what is being said, but in reality the phrase has a double meaning. The first interpretation is to state the opposite: everything is complicated. The second interpretation is that nothing, whatever it may be, is simplistic, clear, easy to understand. Regardless of which explanation one chooses, nothing is being described. Not only does this statement ascribe nothing a *state of existence,* but, in this example, that state is described as "simple." I wondered how this was possible, leading me to ask myself, "How is nothing truly defined?"

The dictionary defines *nothing* as "not any thing: no thing." Since it is a defined word with meaning, it seems that nothing actually is something. Something with significance and a necessary role in our universe. But what kind of role does "not any thing" have? Is nothing truly the absence of all things? I don't think so.

What is it you think of when you hear the word *nothing*? A void? Empty space? These things often came to my mind, but the flaw in these perceptions is that empty holes and space are things that can be described and defined and thus are also *things* rather than *no things*. Another definition of *nothing* is "zeros with the black edges rubbed off." But is this true? Thoughts of this nature led me on a further quest for observations and answers. I started to look at my own human experience with the word *nothing*.

I have always been fascinated with numbers, and my field of work as a pathologist demanded some mathematical proficiency, so naturally my mind considered the numerical nothing. Zero. As one example, on a number line or sequence, when we travel from positive numbers to negative numbers, we have to pass through zero, which is representative of nothing. This one number may truly be nil, but it is still definable as a number and is absolutely necessary in mathematics and our daily lives. In fact, think about it: if zero is nothing, then the minus or negative numbers are defined as less than zero or less than nothing, therefore zero has to be something! Do negative numbers really define anything? Let's use cookies. We understand what two is if we have two cookies, and we understand if we have none; but how can there possibly be a negative two cookies? What if we teach the concept of $(-2) + 2 = 0$ by taking known cookies from someone else. Even a child can understand the positive 2 and taking 2 to reach 0 cookies, but if we give the negative 2 child two cookies, and then tell him he now has none, he will look at those two cookies and know we are crazy. The fact remains that zero as nothing, and negative numbers as less than nothing, are a mystery but yet are real entities in the world of mathematics.

When I was a kid, my mom or dad often interrupted my play or mischief and asked me what I was doing. My default response, as is common with most children, was "nothing." Even though both my parents and I were well aware that I was up to something, an unspoken understanding existed that the nothing I was doing was something I did not want to share.

Also, it was not uncommon for boys of my time to respond to a demonstration by one of our buddies with the phrase, "Oh, that was nothing!" We defined the trick or talent as nothing, but in reality our friend had done something we didn't find very impressive, or that we thought we could do better. So even as a child, I never thought of nothing as the absence of everything.

As a young man I sometimes said that I'd accomplished something "in nothing flat." Well, think about that phrase. Was I saying that I had completed a task or reached a goal with no time elapsed? When we think still more deeply, we know that something has to be in the "nothing flat" to get us from point A to point B. In our minds we hold the idea of being done or arriving somewhere instantly when our logic knows we only did something quickly.

We use the expression "start with nothing," but we really mean that we are starting with meager means or at a defined point. We talk about getting nothing done when we accomplish little, but we still accomplished something. We say that an item cost us nothing when the price is cheap. We say that something or even a person means nothing to us when we are actually avoiding our feelings of dislike or association with painful experiences.

~

Take my life and let it be
Consecrated, Lord, to Thee.
Take my moments and my days,
Let them flow in endless praise.

Take my hands and let them move
At the impulse of Thy love.
Take my feet and let them be
Swift and beautiful for Thee.

Take my voice and let me sing,
Always, only for my King.
Take my lips and let them be
Filled with messages from Thee.

Take my silver and my gold,
Not a mite would I withhold.
Take my intellect and use
Every pow'r as Thou shalt choose.

Take my will and make it Thine,
It shall be no longer mine.
Take my heart, it is Thine own,
It shall be Thy royal throne.

Take my love, my Lord, I pour
At Thy feet its treasure store.
Take myself and I will be
Ever, only, all for Thee.

— Frances R. Havergal, 1874

~

He who planted the ear, does He not hear? He who formed the eye, does He not see?

— Psalm 94:9

~

All I have seen teaches me to trust the Creator for all I have not seen.

— Ralph Waldo Emerson

We only hear because God provided us with complex ears that can capture the sounds and the even greater complexity in our brains to process and understand the mix of sounds and pauses. So, too, it is with our God-given eyes to see light and process forms and images, even with motion.

2. There Is Nothing in the World

Besides the Bible, creation speaks clearest of God's truth because it so closely reflects the Master Creator, Artist, and Composer of the universe. And the message that creation speaks is this: "Nothing" is significant. It does have a purpose in all of life, and examples exist everywhere in the natural world to confirm this truth.

Cold

We call something cold, but really cold is only the absence of heat. Though we define absolute zero, it is just the limits to the absence of heat that we know and understand. In fact, depending on what the temperature is and how we feel at that moment, we describe conditions in a relative manner of how we feel, as warm (more heat) or cold (less heat). At absolute zero, by definition, we have everything above that point being heat. But, there indeed may be even less heat beyond that zero. So, does cold truly exist, or is it nothing?

Darkness

Another example: Is darkness nothing? Darkness is defined best as the complete absence of light. The Bible has verses that tell us that in God there is no darkness at all, as He is light. Light dispels darkness, but darkness cannot dispel light. We can switch on and off light but not darkness. We can see a star in the dark sky that is millions of light years away, but we cannot distinguish or see the same-size spot of darkness. Darkness is the absence of light, but even the darkness is light to God (see John 1:5 and Psalm 139:12). Again, a condition of seemingly complete absence is something!

Atomic Structure

Let us also examine the very fabric of created things, the building blocks of all things, atoms and molecules. Nothing is sometimes described as "no thing," but oftentimes what we considered as "no thing" was simply undiscovered or undetected at that time. Let me give an example. In our living and nonliving world, we have a current understanding of the atomic and molecular structure of elements that has much more detail and understanding than in previous centuries (or even since my childhood). Each molecule is described as being made up of atomic particles with space in between that contains nothing. Some would argue that we should avoid this assumption because science continues to discover particles within the area of seeming nothingness.

Our most recent tests and studies have not yet found anything in the infinitesimal small and seemingly empty spaces between atoms. What is between the particles? We call it nothing, but think of the disastrous outcome that removing that space would ensue! That empty space may seem to be nothing, but the Lord purposefully made it (and whatever it contains) absolutely necessary to the makeup of an entire existence. In His hands, that nothing makes a difference.

> The earth is the LORD's and all that is in it.
>
> — Psalm 24:1 NRSV

If we consider this further, we realize that this *space of nothingness* is vital for more than the separation of particles alone. It also allows for other forces and energies—gravitational pull, light, sound waves, and much, much more—to exist and to be acted on, seen, felt, and heard. Is there another way to describe the electron shells that are usually drawn as little particles within "energy" orbits or "electron shells" around the nucleus with seemingly nothing in the space between? Because the flying or circling around takes energy, and the electrons are often "stable" and hold their charge and any energy, it is probably better to think of the electrons as a force or field of continuous potential or stored energy "state" (we call it a negative charge) that somehow occupies what we thought was that "empty space" we considered to be nothing.

Outer Space

We often say that outer space represents nothing; however, the mere fact that we define it and use the word *space* indicates that it is there and proves that it is indeed something (that takes up space!). I had a conversation with a pastor friend of mine, Carl Robbins, and he saw this very concept in his own experience. He spoke of an air show in which planes flew about and performed awe-inspiring aerobatic maneuvers. While it seemed that the planes were free to roam about the open air, a defined "box" in the sky with invisible borders limited where they could fly qualifying maneuvers. Though the crowd could not see the box, it was there, defined by coordinates within airspace.

In the same way, the nothingness of space is "observed" and defined by surrounding objects, coordinates, and forces. Just because something is not seen or understood completely doesn't mean it isn't present and does not exist. The vast outer space and universe is full of seeming emptiness we consider nothing, yet the locations of planets and stars and galaxies are precisely located and moving within the so-called emptiness, defining it by parameters of distance between heavenly bodies in light years, as well as the entities and waves that pass through it. The emptiness is not devoid of at least purpose (and therefore is not nothing, in the sense of not anything at all).

Waves: Nothing Changes!

What about waves of water, sound, electricity, energy— and the nothingness I saw within them? Light waves allow sight, and sound waves allow hearing—as well as various other electromagnetic waves that provide energy and electric power. Waves have existed from the beginning of the world. In Genesis the Holy Spirit is described as hovering or quivering over the waters. The stillness of hovering alternated with the steady movement of quivering is much like the activity of energy waveforms that God created to give everything needed for the physical earth as well as life and breath. There is motion with a rise to the height, an instant of stillness, and then motion again with a fall to the depths of the wave. Rise and fall. Rise and fall. Even the pulse of a human heart, literally the heartbeat itself, has a waveform that causes the heart to pause for times of inactivity or nothing so that the organ can alternately fill and pump blood to the body as it was designed to do. But in the pause—in that moment of sheer potential energy before the repetitious rise or fall of the wave begins again—can we actually say that nothing is happening if that moment is crucial to the process? Indeed not! (Did I just use "not," another word for nothing that means something?)

Ocean Tides

First, let us describe waves visible to the naked eye: the ocean waves and the tides. Briefly, an ocean wave at its height is neither swelling nor falling but, rather, has completely stopped to change directions. It makes a 180-degree turn and reverses with a force that matches what it just completed. But for that instant of "nothingness," in the height or valley of the wave, there is only potential energy—but energy nevertheless within that point of nothing. So, too, with the tides. A similar pause occurs when all the waves have come ashore and stretched water out as far as it can on the sand, and then the inward movement pauses (actually stops!) to change directions and the tide falls. We even give a name to that instant of nothingness; we call it high tide, so the nothing is really something!

Electric Current

Waves of alternating current electricity also have their own share of nothing but are more difficult to explain. Like the waves of the ocean, these waveforms also have a point of neither rising or falling. Flowing down a wire at say sixty cycles per second, alternating current, or AC electricity, is both an electric field (we call voltage) with directions and a flow of magnetic charge (we call current). For this type of electricity, the up part of the curve is the positive part of the wave, while the down part of the curve is the negative part of the wave, allowing efficient flow of electricity and maintaining its energy until needed. Typically we think of the electric current flowing in only one direction, but in semiconductors and fluorescent lamps, the electricity waves are actually positive and negative charges flowing in opposite directions at the same time. (I asked myself, "Are there really two nothings working at the same time, as a wave moves up and down and sometimes even the current moves back and forth?") Again, those infinitesimal amounts of nothing prove to be quite important to the energy source that powers our world utilities and technology.

Sound

Sound waves also intrigue me. Like other members of the wave family, sound waveforms have their own nothingness that proves critical to hearing a bird sing, a symphony, speech, and laughter. And my curiosity also was piqued when I read a report of sound waves coming at one another from opposite directions, almost like jousting competitors. This convergence of equal forces can produce a zone where there is no transfer of energy, creating what is called a "standing wave." Energy stands on all sides, pushing against, but nothing is in the center of the standing or stationary wave. Somehow, in this center zone, a water drop can be suspended indefinitely! Something (the waveform force) is working in the nothing and holding the water drop stationary from all sides. The nothing *state* created out of the opposite but equal activity of these sound waves actually has a purpose and an effect on drops of liquid. Is this area of seeming nothing truly nothing after all?

Music

One of the most marvelous things that a sound wave can produce is music. What I had never considered before (as I listened to my wife play the piano or my children sing "Happy Birthday" to me) is that music is a series of somethings called notes and nothings called rests.

In music, a whole note is held down for four beats. Because each quarter note is held for one beat, four quarter notes is equivalent to one whole note. But think for a minute. How does our brain distinguish the difference between the whole note and four quarter notes if they are both four beats long and the same sound? There are brief gaps of change and even silence between the quarter notes that separate them. It is the lack of sound in between—the nothing—that makes the difference!

The same concept can be seen with musical rests. A rest is a small, selected span of time in which no sound is played or heard. On the music score, these gaps of no sound are strategically placed within the music through symbols for this nothing. Without the carefully arranged individual notes and rests, only continuous sound is heard. This is not music. A world without nothing would be a world without "Minuet in G" or "Amazing Grace." A world without nothing is a world without music! Again, nothing is a necessary something, and in this case is silence.

Louie Giglio has shared his passion for God's greatness by giving many talks about how space containing the stars with their pulsars (intermittent radio wave pulses) sing and give glory to God in the heavens. All nature sings the symphony of our God with silence and sound. Pulsars provide glorious music as "the heavens declare the glory of God" (Psalm 19:1). And "there are heavenly bodies and earthly bodies, but the glory of the heavenly is of one kind, and the glory of the earthly is of another. There is one glory of the sun, and another glory of the moon, and another glory of the stars; for star differs from star in glory" (1 Corinthians 15:40–41).

Think about how you sing and comprehend music. Singing is a series of carefully arranged tones, rhythms, and human sounds mixed with intervals of silence. Without those intervals, individual words and notes could not be distinguished. It is God's amazing design that nothing must be used in order to sing of His glory and grace. Or, indeed, to understand spoken words of conversation with each other!

Vibrations/Tuning: Sympathetic Nothing!

The music world also has sympathetic strings. When a vibrating object is near another still object that is tuned to either the same note or an octave different, the second begins to vibrate without being touched! This can occur with lesser distinction with other harmonious notes. Over the centuries, many instruments have incorporated extra hidden strings to produce this phenomenon. Others have dampers to prevent it. As an example, you can perceive this easiest on a piano. When you first play "middle C," you hear only that note, and it stops when you release the key because dampers are on all the strings. Now slowly depress the octave above (high C), and play the middle C again, fairly loudly. If you listen carefully, you will hear both notes an octave apart! To make this obvious, do the same again, but this time, strike the middle C but immediately release as you continue to keep the high-C key depressed. Consequently, you will only hear high C, and that note, too, will immediately stop when you release its key as the strings are damped again to their resting phase. Because the one note an octave different is doing nothing, it is a perfect candidate to be acted on by the sound of another.

> *Everyone should be quick to listen, slow to speak.*
>
> — James 1:19 NIV

In the same way, we are "in tune" with the Lord because we are made in His image. Because of this, the great Composer can cause the sound of His majesty and glory to be played in us if we only bring nothing. This thought brings us to a crucial question: what is our nothing? How are we to be the notes played and heard, a sympathetic note, or the rests and pauses in His symphony?

We can apply this to our ability to be sympathetic to others. We use the statements, "I am in tune with you," "I hear you on that," "I can lend you a sympathetic ear," and "I feel and share your pain." I am convinced that this natural sound phenomenon has a spiritual aspect that is easily seen. We show sympathy even when we have not gone through the same difficulty. We simply cannot fully understand what the other person is going through, but, if we are *in tune*, we can *feel* the "vibes" and can *hear* the process resounding in our head on the same or a different frequency. God has given us ears to hear: "He who planted the ear, does He not hear?" (Psalm 94:9). We only hear because God provided us with complex ears that can capture the sounds and the even greater complexity in our brains to process and understand the mix of sounds and pauses, but He also allows us to hear sympathetic notes and harmony, both physically and spiritually.

Where Are We Going with All of This?

Theologically where does this land us? What does observing the definition, human experience, and creation teach us about how God views nothing? First, the Lord has given us the ability to understand nothing is something even though we may never be able to completely comprehend it. He gives us the ability to perceive, but we can only make a feeble attempt to break into bite-sized pieces some of the completeness and awesomeness of His concepts. These jumbled pieces, like puzzle pieces, often keep us from completely seeing the whole. Second, what God has allowed us to understand is this: nothingness, or the seeming lack of something, is what might allow the existence and flourishing of other parts of His creation. The light seems brightest and is detected easiest in the dark, and sounds are heard more clearly when they break utter silence. *Therefore, with God, no thing is wasted; or to say it differently, "nothing" is not wasted or useless.*

With this realization we now need to confront our need to not only observe nothingness and emptiness as a part of everything around us but also to apply this concept as a reality in life on this earth as we serve Christ. All of these musings seem to propose that we mirror the Creator, to make sure we not only avoid wasting our nothing but also use this nothing for the Lord. Because nothingness can be found all over creation, surely it must also have a part to play in our lives. If God has intentions for darkness, silence, empty space, cold, and stillness, He must have a purpose for our nothingness as well.

But what is a human's *nothing*? And what does it look like to steward nothing well? To answer this question, we must go to the source, to the very Word of God. That is what we will address in the next chapter. For now read and consider these two translations of 1 Timothy 6:7—"For we brought nothing into the world, and we can take nothing out of it" (NIV), and "For we brought nothing into *this* world, *and it is* certain we can carry nothing out" (NKJV, italics added). It was this simple verse that spurred my search of the Scriptures for nothing, and I believe it is the key to life application as well.

It is more difficult to comprehend and see the quiet or more hidden parts of our world, as we daily face the pace of the busy, hectic, and very obvious.

~

God, who gives life to the dead and calls into being that which does not exist.

— Romans 4:17 NASB

~

"Worthy are you, our Lord and God,
to receive glory and honor and power, for you
created all things, and by your
will they existed and were created."

— Revelation 4:11

God is self-existent and has no limits and is always holy and set apart. God is eternal and has no beginning and no end. He is Yahweh, the ever-present I AM.

3. Finding Nothing in the Bible

Unlike many worldly authors whose original purpose may never be discovered because that purpose died with the author, God reveals His intent to His children who read His Word. His desire is that His readers understand and see His purpose. Not only does He give His followers an effective Teacher in the Holy Spirit, but He also repeats His messages many times and in various ways so that we might progressively understand His truth.

In the Beginning: Nothing!

After looking at all the material presented in chapter 2, I was captivated with the idea of how nothing is important to all things, including our world and human life. I returned to working through the use of Hebrew and Greek words denoting the concept of nothing in Scripture. The Bible uses words we translate as "nothing" more than 250 times and numerous other similar translated words. Through studying the many uses, nothing in Scripture came to have great meaning to me, and thus I hope to you.

> *Let Your work be shown to Your servants, and Your glorious power to their children. Let the favor of the Lord our God be upon us, and establish the work of our hands upon us; yes, establish the work of our hands!*
>
> — Psalm 90:16–17

One could write exhaustively of the various meanings and uses of the words for nothing in the Old and New Testament. As a layman, I seek the Lord's help to observe, understand, and apply the truths in His Word. Again, I remind you that we cannot fully fathom God's concept of nothing because we are not God. But we can see the results in His creation, make judgments or interpretations; and through His allowed finite observations, we are able to learn if nothing shows all mankind a part of how God would have us live on this earth.

For the purpose of this book, we will take a brief look at some Greek and Hebrew definitions and then the biblical usage and concepts in many verses found scattered throughout the pages of God's Word. May the Lord use this limited study for our good and His glory.

Thread of Nothing

Let me start with a caveat that I think is true: Scripture never uses a word for the true absence of anything and everything. We often speak of God creating ex nihilo—out of nothing or from "not anything"—in the sense that we most often think of "nothing" as "absolutely not anything at all." We do understand the universe was nothing in the sense of "nonexistent" until God created it, and then absolutely all the elements were part of it. But, look at the start of the Bible and see the first words, "In the beginning, God created . . . ." We see "beginning," "God," and "created." "In the beginning" is a single Hebrew word with the sense of first and start, while "created" is in the sense of fashion, form, or shape.

In the New Testament, we have another verse that helps us understand creation. Hebrews 11:3 says, "By faith we understand that the universe was created by the word of God, so that what is seen was not made out of things that are visible." The word *created* is translated "framed" in some versions and means perfected, perfectly joined together, prepared; but again, we do not see a word to describe the not anything at all. Instead, we see the words "not made," which in the Greek mean "not come into existence" or "not begin to be." This is followed by "out of things that are visible," which in the Greek means "to shine forth or appear." I believe that the process of God creating can only be understood by faith and is not something we can explain further.

The term *ex nihilo* is Latin for "from or out of nothing." We might state this as "out of not anything at all" or "out of nonexistent." The term is not used in the Bible; however, the Christian concept is that God, as transcendent, eternal, uncreated, and self-existent, created everything that is, out of nothing (in the sense of not anything at all). The word created in Genesis 1 is a Hebrew word for God's creative activity alone, including His speaking even such things as darkness into existence. See also Isaiah 45:7; John 1:3; Hebrews 11:3; and 2 Peter 3:5.

Throughout history many have attempted to have words describe the state of "not anything at all." We use various words of which *nothing* is the most common; however, we really have adopted the word to describe what (something) we do not comprehend or understand. Other uses of the word *nothing* only indicate things and situations that are stripped down, or are nearly naked, to the level we cannot detect, understand, or comprehend. At times mankind perceives and begins to understand at least a part of what was previously thought to be "nothing" or "no thing."

Matthew Henry's commentary on Genesis 1:1–2 reads,

> The first verse of the Bible gives us a satisfying and useful account of the origin of the earth and the heavens. The faith of humble Christians understands this better than the fancy of the most learned men. From what we see of heaven and earth, we learn the power of the great Creator. . . . The Son of God, one with the Father, was with him when he made the world; nay, we are often told that the world was made by him, and nothing was made without him. Oh, what high thoughts should there be in our minds, of that great God whom we worship, and of that great Mediator in whose name we pray! And here, at the beginning of the sacred volume, we read of that Divine Spirit, whose work upon the heart of man is so often mentioned in other parts of the Bible. Observe, that at first there was nothing desirable to be seen, for the world was without form, and void; it was confusion, and emptiness. In like manner the work of grace in the soul is a new creation: and in a graceless soul, one that is not born again, there is disorder, confusion, and every evil work: it is empty of all good, for it is without God; it is dark, it is darkness itself: this is our condition by nature, till Almighty grace works a change in us.

We are all part of His creation. If, like me, you know that as a Christian you were chosen in Christ before the foundation of the earth (Ephesians 1:4), then you might also believe that when God created the earth and all things, He somehow created you and knew you and all that you are. Before we existed on this earth as human beings, we often think of ourselves as nothing. Some also believe that He set us apart before we were born. Although we were nonexistent from a human and earthly perspective, even in this state of nothingness, in some manner we were actually predestined persons. When God gave us our earthly existence at conception and beyond, to our perceived nothingness He added our physical bodies, minds, personalities, emotions, gifts, abilities, weaknesses; and then later, relationships, material possessions, knowledge, and understanding. And, just as the elements of the earth were present for man and woman to be formed, it wasn't until God added His breath of life that we are "human" beings created in His image. During our earthly life we need yet another God-given addition to reach our full potential: a saving relationship with Christ.

> *We are created and made in the image of God who gives us our soul and body, which are part of our earthly life.*

Before we were conceived, we simply did not exist, even though I believe that from the foundation of the world, the foreknowledge of God knew we would exist. Thus, we can confirm in Scripture that God chose us in Him before the foundation of the world (Ephesians 1:4). Scripture also teaches us that we have a distinct soul or spirit that is separate from our body (and when we die, our soul is immediately in the presence of the Lord). For many hundreds of years, there has been a debate as to when we receive our soul. Three views have been proposed. One is preexistent, proposing that our souls exist in heaven long before our conception, and is difficult to support. A preexistent soul describes our soul somehow being part of God's creation from the beginning (but not part of God, and souls are not eternal beings). Another view is called traducianism, proposing that we inherit our soul and body from our parents. I favor a third view called creationism, proposing that God creates a new soul for each person that is given at conception. We are created and made in the image of God, who gives us our soul and body, which are part of our earthly life. At death, our body is in the grave and our soul in the presence of God. At the second coming of Jesus Christ, our new body is reunited with our soul in the new heavens and the new earth for the rest of all eternity.

Soul. The Hebrew word most used for soul is *nephesh* (Strong's 5315) with a root meaning of "breathing out" and seems to have the idea of the means of making a physical body a being. Two other Hebrew words of similar usage are translated as "heart" and "spirit." The Greek word most commonly used is *psyche* (Strong's 5590). As in English, the context is important as the meaning can be a human being with the breath of life or the seat of inner emotions (also can be termed the heart or spirit). Lastly, it can be an essence that differs from the body. Instances in Hebrew for this last meaning include 1 Kings 17:21, "And he stretched himself upon the child three times, and cried unto the LORD, and said, O LORD my God, I pray thee, let this child's soul come into him again" (KJV); and Genesis 35:18, "And as her soul was departing (for she was dying)."

For the Greek word for soul, some of Thayer's Lexicon meanings are:

"that in which there is life; a living being, a living soul; the soul

1. the seat of the feelings, desires, affections, aversions (our heart, soul, etc.)

2. the (human) soul in so far as it is constituted that by the right use of the aids offered it by God it can attain its highest end and secure eternal blessedness, the soul regarded as a moral being designed for everlasting life

3. the soul as an essence which differs from the body and is not dissolved by death (distinguished from other parts of the body)."

God has given us an immortal soul, which came from God and goes to God. Together with our new bodies all Christians will spend eternity with God.

This doctrine of the soul is of great importance. If we do not believe in a soul, then it is "eat, drink, and be merry, for tomorrow we die" kind of belief, and we see no consequence for our deeds. As Christians, we believe as humans we are created in the image of God, body and soul. Our soul will be in the presence of the Lord at the moment of our death and then reunited with our resurrected new body.

Going back to Genesis 1, we see a few verses later the earth is termed "formless and void." That sounds a lot like nothing to our minds, but instead it is describing something beyond our ability to define, as the earth is certainly present and contains something at that time. We could go on to a number of other words similar to *nothing*, and I will mention a few later; but for now, let us concentrate only on nothing, the subject of this book. I will not even pretend to be able to explain or provide a proper exegesis on the wealth of nothing within pages of Scripture. However, I can share a taste of the Greek and Hebrew translation that helped me in understanding the concept of nothing in the Scriptures.

The English translations of the original words we translate as "nothing" can be summarized as follows:

In the Old Testament Hebrew: not any, never, neither let, not anything, not anything left over, bereaved or childless, free (without cause), without cost, lack no thing, not anything remaining.

In the New Testament Greek: not anything, abolish, cease, put an end to, destroy, make void, make of no effect, naught, not, do away with, and interestingly, no man and no one.

Reading through the Bible, one will see these words and phrases sprinkled all over the written Word. At first glance I have often passed over some words and parts of sentences within passages of the Bible without much thought. But I know, and have been taught, that each word is important and specifically intended by God for His purposes. After reading through the Bible each year for more than twenty-five years and participating in or teaching many inductive studies, I discovered that by looking closely at the meaning of biblical words, I was given a new dimension of under- standing. Certainly, each word, as used in its original language and context, is critical to our understanding.

In the Old Testament, two words for nothing are used most frequently. One example is Genesis 11:6 where the actual Hebrew two-word structure is "not" plus "be restrained." The English Standard Version translates as "nothing that they propose to do." Another example is Isaiah 40:17, with a more complex Hebrew word structure: "nothing" plus "before Him" plus "nothing—in the sense of ceasing, ending, final" plus "emptiness, empty space or empty place." The ESV translates as "nothing before Him, they are accounted by Him as less than nothing and emptiness."

In the New Testament, let's observe the verse that I believe may be the key to identifying our own nothing as well as understanding the significance of nothing in Scripture. In 1 Timothy 6:7, various translations state we "bring nothing into the world" and "it is certain we can take nothing out of the world." Both phrases mean nothing, but in some translations, the second phrase is translated "cannot take anything." The Greek words show a slight but interesting difference. Strong's Concordance reveals the first "nothing" is the word *ouden,* which means "no one, nothing, no man." The second "nothing" or "cannot take anything" is the word *oude,* a more forceful expression, as if to say to the reader, "It is a fact that you brought nothing into the world, and you *most certainly* cannot carry even the slightest thing out, no matter what you may have possessed!" I also want you to think about the use of "no one" or "no man" as valid substitute interpretations of these Greek words for nothing.

Let's move on. The above phrases, "nothing" and "not anything," and their usage became catalysts of thought for me. Think! God has us bring nothing with us as we come into the world and also take nothing out. Because of earlier observations I knew already that different perspectives were at my fingertips. The first was the usual human comprehension of nothing showing me the obvious truth that I was born and will die with my hands emptied of all material possessions. But the thought that kept me from stopping with only this basic understanding was this: Do we really come and leave this earthly existence with nothing or even "nothing at all"? So many times I have observed that nothing actually is a necessary something within the world. I had to know if the same was true in Scripture and about each of us.

So I pressed on in study and prayer, including my previous noting that those same Greek words (*ouden, oude*) in some passages were translated as "no man" or "no one." I am not a Greek scholar, but it seems that looking at 1 Timothy 6:7 in light of these additional translation possibilities also shows us something interesting. Not only do we "bring" nothing into this world, but consider whether we could be this "nothing" or "no one"? The same could apply when we "take" as we leave the world. We will bring and take nothing, or our "no man," by and because of our Creator and almighty God.

My first thought was *Can this be true?* Is this the something I was looking for? Let's continue our journey and think through a few more Scriptures. But first, let me give to you the conclusion I propose for what our nothing might be: the "soul" of man.

> Please note that, while I want you to consider your soul as the "nothing" or "no one"—as plausible as that might seem—and I attempt to defend, it is nevertheless an interpretation and not something I can be dogmatic about in any sense. I also want you to understand that word substitution of this nature is often not the best hermeneutical practice. I pray it is not speculation. My desire is to have you think, pray, and study the depths of the riches of our God and His plan for you—all that you think, say, and do while He has you inhabiting this earth.

Hopefully, you will see as I did, the life-changing truths that surfaced when I threaded together the

Scriptures that follow in the next chapter. It would mean that your nothing that you came into the world with, your soul, is at the very core of your life on this earth. With the components of our earthly life that God adds to it, and then the addition of our knowing Him, we are also given an opportunity and responsibility not to waste this nothing. I desire that God's Word challenge you to think deeper and apply His truth for proper use of your life. With Jesus as our Savior and Lord, our Treasure, and the direction of the Holy Spirit in our lives, only then can we properly use our nothing for His glory. Otherwise, we will be useless to our Master and Creator.

~

O Love that wilt not let me go, I rest my weary
    soul in thee;
I give thee back the life I owe, . . .
O Light that followest all my way, I yield my
    flickering torch to thee;
My heart restores its borrowed ray, . . .
               —George Matheson, 1882

~

"For whoever wishes to save his life will lose it;
but whoever loses his life for My sake will find
it. For what will it profit a man if he gains the
whole world and forfeits his soul? Or what will
a man give in exchange for his soul?"
               — Matthew 16:25–26 NASB

~

There are heavenly bodies and earthly bodies,
but the glory of the heavenly is of one kind,
and the glory of the earthly is of another. There
is one glory of the sun, and another glory
of the moon, and another glory of the stars;
for star differs from star in glory. So is it with
the resurrection of the dead. What is sown is
perishable; what is raised is imperishable. It is
sown in dishonor; it is raised in glory. It is sown
in weakness; it is raised in power. It is sown
a natural body; it is raised a spiritual body. If
there is a natural body, there is also a spiritual
body. Thus it is written, "The first man Adam
became a living being"; the last Adam became
a life-giving spirit. But it is not the spiritual that
is first but the natural, and then the spiritual.
The first man was from the earth, a man of
dust; the second man is from heaven. As was
the man of dust, so also are those who are of
the dust, and as is the man of heaven, so also
are those who are of heaven. Just as we have
borne the image of the man of dust, we shall
also bear the image of the man of heaven.

— 1 Corinthians 15:40–49

~

Blessed be the God and Father of our Lord
Jesus Christ, who has blessed us in Christ
with every spiritual blessing in the heavenly
places, even as He chose us in Him before the
foundation of the world, that we should be
holy and blameless before Him.

— Ephesians 1:3–4

~

God, who saved us and called us to a holy
calling, not because of our works but because
of His own purpose and grace, which He gave
us in Christ Jesus before the ages began.
— 2 Timothy 1:8–9

~

For from Him and through Him and to Him are
all things. To Him be glory forever. Amen.
— Romans 11:36

~

We truly are from Him as He is our Creator.
When we are saved, we belong; we are in Him
and He in us. He works through us. One day we
will go back to Him where we will dwell in His
glorious presence forever.

~

An August 2008 blog entry entitled "Everything to Nothing" by Tim Challies (www.timchallies.com) included an interesting comparison of Abraham Lincoln rising from backwoods rail splitter to president, contrasting the opposite kind of process in Philippians 2 about Christ being everything and becoming nothing.

Challies states, "Though Jesus Christ was 'in the form of God, [he] did not count equality with God a thing to be grasped, but made himself nothing, taking the form of a servant, being born in the likeness of men' (Philippians 2:6,7). Jesus had been exalted far beyond the office of president. He was in the form of God; He was God. And yet He humbled Himself far lower than a rail splitter living in a squalid little cabin miles from nowhere. '[B]eing found in human form, he humbled himself by becoming obedient to the point of death, even death on a cross.'"

G od's Word is Truth and the standard of measure; our understanding and application is fallible.

4. Sampling of Scriptures

As we continue in Genesis, we see the negative or wasted use of nothing in the lives of unbelievers who are in rebellion against God. One instance is Genesis 11:6, where the triune God is discussing man at the tower of Babel and saying, "and now nothing which they propose to do will be impossible for them" (NASB). They were adding to and using their nothing for self-serving glory. So God confused their language to end their perfect communication. But why? Why would God hinder the unity of man in this way? For the simple fact that a tower erected for the exaltation of man can only end in pride and destruction and leads to ultimate separation from God. They were aiming for heaven, but they would have quickly found themselves in hell. One could say God was merciful here. All of the added intelligence, skill, and strength would have left them with only their nothing in the end. All of them would have left this earth with their nothing and continued in eternity as lost souls, separated from God forever.

In Genesis 40:15 Joseph says of his being sold into slavery, "I have done nothing that they should put me into the pit." This is not his way of claiming inaction (not doing anything), but instead he is saying I have not done anything worthy of punishment. Indeed, the phrase is "done nothing," and in order to "do nothing," it has to be something! This is a passage that teaches us we, too, can do many things, but they may be counted as worthless, as not anything worthwhile, when held up to a certain end result standard, desired or not. In the same way, when facing a test, a student who does many things during the course of the day but doesn't study may say he or she accomplished nothing.

Exodus

Exodus 12:20 states regarding the Passover meal, "You shall eat nothing leavened." Interestingly, "eat nothing" is again meant to signify something! Nothing here encompasses all things that are leavened. It is not used as the absence of all things but rather to represent many things.

Concerning a Hebrew slave who was bought and served his master for six years, Exodus 21:2 says, "and in the seventh year he shall go out free, for nothing." Although this is meant in terms of no payment or other redemption, this slave who did not have anything of status or wealth could leave, for nothing, or remain to become a bondservant. A slave who became a bond-slave declared to the world that being a nobody and having nothing with his master was everything to him. His seeming nothingness gave great value to his life.

Psalms

Because of our hope of eternal life with Christ, my wife and I often had honest discussions about difficulties, trials, her brain cancer, and dying. We wanted to glorify God by doing and finishing all things well. In Psalm 62, several verses call attention to the importance of resting (remember my music example of rests) and trusting in the Lord and His power through those times. The following verses propose that those seasons of rest that might seem like times of dryness or nothing are really full of potential for God to do something great! The verses of Psalm 62 that I see suggesting this concept read as follows:

> 1–2: For God alone my soul waits in silence; from him comes my salvation. He only is my rock and my salvation, my fortress; I shall not be greatly shaken.
> 5–10: For God alone, O my soul, wait in silence, for my hope is from him. He only is my rock and my salvation, my fortress; I shall not be shaken. On God rests my salvation and my

glory; my mighty rock, my refuge is God. Trust
in him at all times, O people; pour out your heart
before him; God is a refuge for us. Selah. Those
of low estate are but a breath; those of high estate
are a delusion; in the balances they go up; they
are together lighter than a breath. Put no trust in
extortion; set no vain hopes on robbery; if riches
increase, set not your heart on them.

11–12: Once God has spoken; twice have I
heard this: that power belongs to God, and that
to you, O Lord, belongs steadfast love.

In the first two verses, the psalmist reminds us
that our soul is to stop, wait, or rest in God alone who
provides salvation—even through seemingly endless
times when God appears to be doing nothing and any
potential blessing is masked. (Read this last sentence
again and see a phrase we often use, "doing nothing,"
which, merely in the saying, has to mean something!)
Then in verses 5 and 6 the psalmist repeats the concept,
this time commanding us to wait or rest in those times
of "nothing." We are to reflect on the certainty of the
potential good and hope that comes from God alone,
no matter the wait. We are not to try to do anything in
ourselves, no matter the feeling of "emptiness." Finally,
verses 11 and 12 tell us that we have now been told
twice that the potential that appears to be nothing
is really power that belongs to God. It is a steadfast,
loving God who decides when His power will be manifested and the potential hope made a reality, especially
as it is manifested in our lives.

I have seen these truths applied in my own life and struggles. He provided more opportunities for both Gini and I to share the gospel in the midst of trials than in many of our Bible studies in years past. This was because of all the people He brought into our path along our difficult journey. God truly allowed good out of seeming nothingness.

In another passage the psalmist expresses that none, no one, notices him or cares for his soul.

> When my spirit faints within me, you know my way! In the path where I walk they have hidden a trap for me. Look to the right and see: there is none who takes notice of me; no refuge remains to me; no one cares for my soul. I cry to you, O LORD; I say, "You are my refuge, my portion in the land of the living." (Psalm 142:3–5)

As we observe the passage, we can see that the word translated as "none" or "no one" is still someone. That someone is just ignoring him or has no ability to notice him. The psalmist goes on then to recognize that the Lord is our refuge and portion in the land of the living (on earth). He, the Omnipotent, the Savior, is not only taking notice of us but watching over us, allowing our souls to "take refuge" in Him. Sometimes I fit right into these words, guilty of not seeing or paying attention to someone who knows me. Instead I am focused on someone else or something else, so that person often has been hurt and sometimes confronted me. In their eyes they think I see them as a nobody.

Do we grieve because we are treated as nothing, are ignored, or made unimportant by another human being? When we feel this way we can remember that we remain nothing until made something by God. And we remember Christ. He made Himself nothing when He came in human form to us.

"I have come that they may have life, and have it to the full."

— John 10:10 NIV

He cares for us and gave His life—His everything—literally to and for us. He took on death that we might have life. We will discuss this more when we discuss Philippians 2.

"Be still and know that I am Lord." This command is found in Psalm 46:10. The Scriptures often display the Lord like a whisper in the stillness, in the absence of all noise and activity. Think back to our discussion of music. Music differs from simple sound because of the organization of sounds and pauses. It is the stillness and pauses that allow us to perceive notes and harmony of music, and not only noise! Thus it is with our relationship with God. We have to be quiet, to be still, to be nothing (yet at the same time something, just absent certain aspects of our being) to know and understand Him and learn who we are. I believe we see that we were created and given life to be a nothing in and of ourselves. Only an empty pitcher can be filled. We were made to be empty as Christ became empty so that we could be filled with His purpose, not ours. We must not be filled with ourselves only!

Let me elaborate a little more on quietness. We often speak of having a "quiet time," yet when we ask someone to discuss what a quiet time is or what he personally does, the answer is far from quiet or still. There is a setting aside of time to be with the Lord, reading verses and passages from the Bible, praying through a set list, and other activities. Sometimes, someone will mention that he includes a time of "meditation." We almost never hear the person say that he is truly quiet and doing nothing to allow the Lord to teach and mold him through His Spirit in his inner being—in stillness. And, no one mentions that he may have even fallen asleep during his morning or evening "quiet time," yet in even those times (and prob-ably more because we are the most quiet), the Lord teaches mightily ("He gives to His beloved even in his sleep," Psalm 127:2 NASB. "For God speaks in one way, and in two, though man does not perceive it. In a dream, in a vision of the night, when deep sleep falls on men, while they slumber on their beds," Job 33:14–15).

> *Now I lay me down to sleep, I pray the Lord my soul to keep. If I should die before I wake, I pray to God my soul to take. If I should live for other days, I pray my Lord to guide my ways.*
>
> —Child's nighttime prayer

Isaiah

In Isaiah 40:17, the Lord says that "All the nations are as nothing before Him, they are accounted by Him as less than nothing and emptiness." In his commentary, Matthew Henry expounds on this verse saying:

> The nations of the world are nothing in comparison of Him. . . . Take them all together, all the great and mighty nations of the earth, kings the most pompous, kingdoms the most populous, both the most wealthy; take the isles, the multitude of them, the isles of the Gentiles: *Before Him*, when they stand in competition with Him or in opposition to Him, they are *as a drop of the bucket* compared with the vast ocean, or *the small dust of the balance* (which does not serve to turn it, and therefore is not regarded, it is so small) in comparison with all the dust of the earth. *He takes them up*, and throws them away from Him, *as a very little thing*, not worth speaking of. They are all in His eye *as nothing*, as if they had no being at all; for they add nothing to His perfection and all-sufficiency. *They are counted by Him*, and are to be counted by us in comparison of Him, *less than nothing, and vanity*. When He pleases, He can as easily bring them all into nothing as at first He brought them out of nothing. (italics added)

In this verse from Isaiah, we know that God could be using nothing in the sense of a hyperbole, an exaggeration, to help us feel the insignificance of the nations to God. But could we look at this another way? If we look carefully, this reference suggests the very real presence of nothing, but it also presents the strange idea of less than nothing! If there is such a thing as "less than nothing," then nothing must be something from which subtraction is possible. Like the mathematical zero and negative numbers, or a darkness beyond utter or outer darkness, this "less than nothing" is a concept that we cannot completely understand. As the Lord says in Isaiah 40:28, "The LORD is the everlasting God, . . . His understanding is unsearchable."

Isaiah 40:21–23 goes on to ask, if we have not understood from the foundations of the earth (taking a clue from creation), "It is He who sits above the circle of the earth; . . . who stretches out the heavens like a curtain, . . . who brings princes to nothing, and makes rulers of the earth as emptiness." I think these verses confirm to us that we continually depend on the God who not only created the world out of things not visible, but we also depend on His work to make something of our nothingness or to leave us useless.

Luke

In Luke 19:26, Christ is telling the crowds the parable of the talents in which the master of the house gives his three servants wages of one, five, and ten minas to manage. When he returns he finds that the servants with ten and five minas have invested and doubled their earnings. He praises and rewards them. To the servant who was given only one mina but did not do anything but hide it away in the ground, he says, "I tell you that to everyone who has, more will be given, but as for the one who has nothing, even what they have will be taken away" (NIV). We see that he was a servant and that did not change, but what was added to him (the mina) was taken away (even what he has)

Only by investing our God-given talents and abilities for God and His kingdom will we make the proper something of our nothing, and it will not be wasted.

as he returned to his base or original state. The servant was stripped of his money and cast out. We come into the world with nothing and leave with nothing. Do you see the unbeliever is naked, poor, and wretched (see Revelation 3:17)—his body and soul spending eternity under the wrath of God without the presence of a Mediator? Although the parable is about differences in earthly investing, I ask you to consider the spiritual or heavenly application as well. Only by investing our God-given talents and abilities for God and His kingdom will we make the proper something of our nothing, and it will not be wasted. You do not want to be left worthless for all eternity.

Unbelievers (unrepentant and unsaved sinners) are not eternally separated from God, as some might describe hell, but they are eternally separated from His blessings, His mercy, and the mediating work of Christ. It is a place of eternal punishment and not the place of eternal blessings, mercy, and fellowship with God. We have Jesus' description of hell as a lake of fire, and it is a place of unending destructive torment without being consumed. Because God is omnipresent, He is even in hell as we see in verses such as Psalm 139:8. Jonathan Edwards referenced Revelation 6:15–16 and said, "Wicked men will hereafter earnestly wish to be turned to nothing and forever cease to be that they may escape the wrath of God." R. C. Sproul described it this way: "Hell, then, is an eternity before the righteous, ever-burning wrath of God, a suffering torment from which there is no escape and no relief." So, hell is the place of all the wrath of God without a Mediator.

Acts

One of the most profound verses on human existence is Acts 17:28—"In Him we live and move and have our being." You are a created being coming into the world empty and with your nothing, and to your seeming humiliation, you will leave the same way. During your life on this earth, God not only gives you a body and breath; He also provides for your every need. You might say you are "value added"! When He takes your breath away, you die and take your *nothing* with you, your very core being that you have in Him.

You have an opportunity, by the grace of God and His provision, to make your soul something of value. As a chosen child of God, you will take that opportunity, responding to His providential call. Only when He changes us can our souls be useful on earth and be clothed in the righteousness of Christ throughout eternity. Others will not respond and will find themselves a tragic waste.

Romans

Romans 6:6 declares, "We know that our old self was crucified with Him in order that the body of sin might be brought to nothing, so that we would no longer be enslaved to sin." Let me use an illustration. You have a "box" filled with sin. Christ died on your behalf that your "box" of sin might be emptied. Although an empty box may be made to look beautiful and worthy of holding valuables, it is empty nonetheless. Through Christ, you put to death all of your own attempts at filling or concealing the void within your "box." Thus you see that Christ made us empty of self-made righteousness and numerous sins, and then that empty box or void (our nothing) is now fit to fill. Or think of this Bible example as the sin that has "clothed" your nothing is removed when you accept Christ as

Lord and Savior. Your sin clothing is stripped away so your nakedness (our nothing) is now clothed with the glorious Treasure (gift) of Jesus Christ in you, the hope of glory, and you truly realize that in Him (and His Spirit within) you live (we call this being born again or new life in Christ) and move and have your being. We are allowed to see we no longer need to "fix" our condition of nothingness. Our nothing is now something in being filled with the Spirit. While on this earth you recognize sin still has some mastery over you, but you rejoice that this sin in you has no lasting power or control in your life.

God's love is everything to the Christian. Without the favor of the Almighty, you have no future, no hope. Praise be to God that once He has chosen to give your soul His love, it can never, no never, be taken away. Romans 8:29 teaches us that in some manner God foreknew and predestined His elect to be conformed to His Son. (Also see Revelation 3:5; 13:8 about our names being written in the Lamb's book of life before the foundation of the world.) In Romans 8:38–39, Paul states emphatically with full confidence, "For I am sure that neither death nor life, nor angels nor rulers, nor things present nor things to come, nor powers, nor height nor depth, nor anything else in all of creation, will be able to separate us from the love of God in Christ Jesus our Lord." Each time the word *nor* appears in the passage, the apostle is actually using the Greek word *oute*, which means "neither, nor, not, yet not." When He gives you His love, He not only promises it eternally, but He also takes your nothing and makes it something useful for the Master's work—the work He has for you to do while on this earth as an alien and stranger. He adds to your soul His value, purpose, election, calling, justification, and glorification— guaranteeing all things work together for our good, according to His will, and for His glory (see Romans 8:28), and thus your nothing soul is not wasted.

Corinthians

First Corinthians 1:28–29 is one of the first passages that inspired my mind and heart to think about *nothing*. Paul says, "God chose what is low and despised in the world, even things that are not, to bring to nothing things that are, so that no human being might boast in the presence of God." But how, I asked myself, can something that "is not" or "nothing" be utilized to do anything, and will be kept from boasting before God? Again we see the power of our God! He created our nothing then reduces our added things to nothing and uses our nothing as something from which He will ultimately receive glory!

In the next chapter Paul says to the Corinthians, "I decided to know nothing among you except Jesus Christ and Him crucified" (1 Corinthians 2:2). I wondered how a person could determine or decide to know nothing. If nothing can be known, it must be something! Isn't this the man who sought in chapter 9 of this same book to become all things to all people to win souls for Christ? How can he be all things when he knows nothing? And what is the nothing that he claims we can know? But then I realized, that just as we empty a drawer to make room for new contents, Paul was saying that he would gladly remove knowledge of all the extra things we add to our nothing souls to make room for more of Christ. A container of nothing is still a container and has the potential to suddenly hold something infinitely precious. By knowing nothing, Paul is doing as he says in Philippians 3:8, "Indeed, I count everything as loss because of the surpassing worth of knowing Christ Jesus my Lord."

In 1 Corinthians 13, the chapter about love, the truth that our souls are nothing apart from the affections of Christ is confirmed: "If I speak in the tongues of men and of angels, but have not love, I am a noisy gong or a clanging cymbal. And if I have prophetic powers, and understand all mysteries and all knowledge, and if I have all faith, so as to remove mountains, but have not love, *I am nothing.* If I give away all I have, and if I deliver up my body to be burned, but have not love, *I gain nothing*" (vv. 1–3, italics added).

Paul, in matter of fact fashion, teaches us that without love we are nothing (our nothing or soul is unloving). And because God is love, it is safe to say that without God we are nothing (not a child of God and not clothed with His righteousness). Simple but potent truth—and even more potent when we think of the waste of our nothing if we are without Christ (God's gift of love to the believer; see John 3:16).

Galatians

Galatians 6:3 introduces another aspect of my proposed concept of nothing. With an edge of warning, Paul writes to the self-righteous Galatians, "For if anyone thinks he is something, when he is nothing, he deceives himself." When we give eternal value to, and think highly of, our self-made additions to our nothing souls, we deceive ourselves. Paul says this to implore his readers to evaluate themselves because people who stay in deceit will remain a naked, unclothed nothing in eternity. Their time in this world and the next will have no God-added clothing. This is the contrast of self-righteous clothing and God-righteous clothing, or said another way, clothed with the righteousness of God.

Philippians

The Scriptures give us the example of Christ who was sent to the earth in the realm and fullness of time and then accomplished the will of His Father. Philippians 2 tells us that Jesus "emptied Himself." Looking at the first part of this chapter gives yet another insight into the concept of nothingness within us.

> So if there is any encouragement in Christ, any
> comfort from love, any participation in the
> Spirit, any affection and sympathy, complete
> my joy by being of the same mind, having the
> same love, being in full accord and of one mind.
> Do *nothing* from selfish ambition or conceit,
> but in humility count others more significant

than yourselves. Let each of you look not only to his own interests, but also to the interests of others. Have this mind among yourselves, which is yours in Christ Jesus, who, though He was in the form of God, did not count equality with God a thing to be grasped, but emptied Himself, by taking the form of a servant, being born in the likeness of men. And being found in human form, He humbled himself by becoming obedient to the point of death, even death on a cross. Therefore God has highly exalted Him and bestowed on Him the name that is above every name, so that at the name of Jesus every knee should bow, in heaven and on earth and under the earth, and every tongue confess that Jesus Christ is Lord, to the glory of God the Father.

Therefore, my beloved, as you have always obeyed, so now, not only as in my presence but much more in my absence, work out your own salvation with fear and trembling, for it is God who works in you, both to will and to work for his good pleasure.

Do all things without grumbling or disputing, that you may be blameless and innocent, children of God without blemish in the midst of a crooked and twisted generation, among whom you shine as lights in the world, holding fast to the word of life, so that in the day of Christ I may be proud that I did not run in vain or labor in vain. Even if I am to be poured out as a drink offering upon the

sacrificial offering of your faith, I am glad and
rejoice with you all. Likewise you also should be
glad and rejoice with me. (Philippians 2:1–18,
italics added)

This passage starts by telling us that we should
seek like-mindedness with fellow believers, but Paul
truly hits home when he teaches that our minds
should be like that of Christ. Paul says we should be
like Jesus Christ who was poured out or emptied, and
so made Himself in some sense nothing, that through
becoming and coming in the form of man, He could
defeat death for us.

> The phrase "emptied Himself" is also translated as
> "made Himself nothing." This phrase is followed by
> three statements: "taking the form," "being born,"
> and "being found." Jesus coming to earth as a human
> does not mean that any of His divine being has been
> removed. Instead, the Reformation Study Bible
> states that Jesus humbled Himself, relinquishing His
> heavenly status, not His divine being. Later in 2 John,
> this study Bible further explains the humanity of
> Jesus is associated with "human limitations of
> hunger (Matthew 4:2), fatigue (John 4:6), ignorance
> of fact (Luke 8:45–47), and sorrow (John 11:35, 38).
> . . . Jesus could not sin, but He was able to be
> tempted . . . . Being human, Jesus could not conquer
> temptation without a struggle, but being divine it
> was His nature to do His Father's will . . . . Since His
> human nature was conformed to His divine nature,
> it was impossible that He should fail."

When the Holy Spirit regenerates us, we are born again. We acknowledge and understand Jesus as our Savior, Lord, and the very gift of God at the time of our salvation. We also begin to understand what He poured out when He emptied Himself, came to earth, died, and was resurrected to redeem His chosen. When, in our very being, we have the Spirit of Christ in our hearts, we are never the same. Then, we have the ability to humble ourselves through the example of Jesus, recognizing ourselves for the nothing we truly are. We then are allowed to share in the glory of Christ, receiving everything He poured out for us.

We often hear and have used the expressions, "Invite Jesus into your heart" and "Jesus lives inside of you." But, in John 14:6, Jesus says, "I am the way, and the truth, and the life," and a little later, in verses 16–17, "[the Father] will give you another Helper, to be with you forever, even the Spirit of truth, whom the world cannot receive, because it neither sees Him nor knows Him. You know Him, for He dwells with you and will be in you." And in John 14:26, we are told, "But the Helper, the Holy Spirit, whom the Father will send in my name, He will teach you all things and bring to your remembrance all that I have said to you." So, believers have the Holy Spirit or the Spirit of Christ indwelling them. See also John 16:4b–15. Jesus came to earth and will come again. Meanwhile, we have His Spirit leading, guiding, and directing our lives.

In Philippians 3, Paul entreats his readers not to glory in their spiritual pedigree. When such a man does boast, he often is prone to be proud of things he has gained (his assets), ignoring that God added them to him. In verses 7 through 12, Paul shows us the proper mind-set saying,

> But whatever gain I had, I counted as loss for the sake of Christ. Indeed, I count everything as loss because of the surpassing worth of knowing Christ Jesus my Lord. For His sake I have suffered the loss of all things and count them as rubbish, in order that I may gain Christ and be found in Him, not having a righteousness of my own that comes from the law, but that which comes through faith in Christ, the righteousness from God that depends on faith—that I may know Him and the power of His resurrection, and may share His sufferings, becoming like Him in His death, that by any means possible I may attain the resurrection from the dead.

In these verses you see that while on this earth, everything you have added to your nothing is not your own (spiritual or material); and even what you do have that could be identified as gain, you should consider as loss (a liability) or *not anything* when compared to knowing Christ. The word *rubbish* can be translated dung, detestable, or worthless. You must have faith in Him, acknowledge Him, and share in His sufferings.

This intimate, relational knowledge of Christ is the key to avoiding a wasted soul—a wasted life. It is He who makes you a vessel of honor, and it is He who fills your empty vessel for His use. (See 2 Timothy 2:20–21.)

~

Significant can be a strange word—used to describe both difficult times of trial and the feelings of worth. Finding significance in God is following Christ every moment of every day, making life worth the living. God's will for our lives includes meaning, reason, and purpose.

~

Now may the God of peace who brought again from the dead our Lord Jesus, the great shepherd of the sheep, by the blood of the eternal covenant, equip you with everything good that you may do his will, working in us that which is pleasing in his sight, through Jesus Christ, to whom be glory forever and ever.

— Hebrews 13:20-21

~

There is a God-shaped vacuum in the heart of every man which cannot be filled by any created thing, but only by God the Creator made known through Jesus Christ.

— Blaise Pascal

~

Until Christ fills our heart, we search the things of this world to fill that hole.

Our souls are not at rest until they find significance in Jesus as Lord and Savior, then seeking to do His will with our earthly body.

5. Something from Nothing

In Latin the name *Nemo* means "nothing, no man, nobody, no one." The word has been found in literature through the ages. It shows up in a Charles Dickens novel, *Bleak House*. In the midst of this dark story, a character signs the ledger as Nemo when he hires out as a copyist; but when he dies, the sad truth is that they really don't know who he is, except seemingly a pauper—a "nobody," an unknown man—until much later revealed. In Jules Verne's *Twenty Thousand Leagues Under the Sea*, Captain Nemo is the fictional character about which little is known or revealed and who says, "I am nothing to you but Captain Nemo." And of course there is the beloved, little lost fish that no one knows anything about, but everyone seeks, in the film *Finding Nemo*.

Finding Nothing

This concept, that the nothingness of humanity can be deeply felt and diligently searched for, is not new under the sun. Whether we admit it outright or show it subconsciously, our soul knows it is totally absent of all else without God. In our search through Scripture, I believe we have finally found our "Nemo." Our soul is brought into the world when we are conceived, knit in the womb, and we become breathing human beings.

It is essential that we understand our resurrection body will be reunited with our soul as we fully enjoy the new heavens and new earth. At the tomb on Easter morning, Mary at first does not know Jesus is standing beside her but then recognizes Him as He speaks to her. Later in John 21, Peter recognizes Jesus, who is on the shore speaking and cooking fish! This is after He died and before He ascended. Somehow, our earthly body that lies in the grave will be raised up at the second coming of our Lord, Jesus Christ; and in the new heaven and the new earth, we will have a new glorified body. Although we are described as free of sin, glorified, new, and changed, we, too, will be recognizable. In some manner, we will dwell body and soul, the rest of all eternity. (See 1 Corinthians 15:35–49.)

When we are physically born, we have a body, mind, abilities, and so much more that God adds to our souls. When we take our last breath, our souls are immediately in the presence of God, and later our body that has rested in the ground will somehow be reunited with our soul for all eternity.

John 15:4–6 are good verses to reflect upon:

"Abide in Me, and I in you. As the branch
cannot bear fruit of itself, unless it abides in the
vine, neither can you, unless you abide in Me.
I am the vine, you are the branches. He who
abides in Me, and I in him, bears much fruit; for
without Me you can do nothing. If anyone does
not abide in Me, he is cast out as a branch and is
withered; and they gather them and throw them
into the fire, and they are burned."

Within His created time and universe, we see God is using "nothing" all around us, as well as in us and through us, while we dwell on this earth—for His purposes and for His glory alone. And, as this occurs, our nothing in the hands of our sovereign God cannot be wasted. He then enables us to recognize and offer our nothing to God, so that our soul's added attributes and abilities turn toward Him.

Once we understand this, once we find the reality of our Nemo, we are faced with a choice. In addition to our God-given body and abilities, will we choose to add and keep what is eternally worthless to our soul? Will we waste our nothing and be as Jonathan Edwards once wrote in *The Justice of God in the Damnation of Sinners* (1734): "A little, wretched, despicable creature; a worm, a mere nothing and less than nothing; a vile insect that has risen up in contempt against the Majesty of heaven and earth"? Or will we choose to seek God's direction during our earthly lives so that we make something, indeed see Him make all things and everything of our nothing in this world and the next?

Finding Significance

After God provides and changes our heart, then we see how He uses us and we find our significance. See 2 Corinthians 5:17–21 and Zechariah 3, but I want to comment especially on Zechariah 3. Although the verses are written to Joshua, most Bible scholars indicate it applies to each Christian, so I will restate the principles as applying to each of us and our Christian walk. Satan is pictured as the accuser and of course is the prince of this world. The Lord rebukes Satan and his influence on us and likens us to a "brand plucked from the fire." We have been removed from the fire, and we are changed to be used in an entirely different way. Next we see the example of being covered in filthy clothes and the command to have those garments removed, so that we are then clothed with pure vestments. Next a reminder that, "If you will walk in my ways and keep my charge, then . . . ," followed a verse later, "behold, I will bring my servant the Branch" (Branch capitalized is a reference to Jesus). Finally, we see the brand (us) removed from the fire is now to brand or place an imprint on others as we invite others to "come under His vine and under His fig tree." Similar to what I did as a child in Nebraska while branding cattle, I am to use my brand, fully heated, to place a brand of the Branch on those around me, to leave an imprint of the Lord. I am to invite others that they might see He is our Lord, Savior, and Treasure who, by His death and resurrection, took away our sin and

After God provides and changes our heart, then we see how He uses us and we find our significance.

provided that we can be changed—we can be plucked from the fire and then be used. What an example of His providing—and our "finding significance."

As you move on to the next chapter, my desire is that you know that your nothing really is something—a nothing that is something of great value to God. Not only that you have found out what your nothing is, but you also find significance in your life through that special relationship with God through Jesus Christ as your Savior, Lord, and very treasured Gift. Pray in the name of Jesus Christ, and ask His Holy Spirit to help you to understand all of the truth in God's Word and then apply it to you for the rest of your life. Join other believers in worship, and share this good news with other people as you walk and talk the remainder of your days of your journey on this earth.

~

My Car

When I arrived, I did not know it was my car,
Provided to me from afar,
Carefully cared for by Mom and Dad,
Not a single care I had.

In a car seat was my place,
Not even to walk, let alone race,
I was comfortable at home,
And had no reason to roam.

As I grew, I recognized the many cars around,
And soon took notice of my own in my surrounds,
I tentatively pushed on the gas pedal a time or two,
But was not to leave the garage with any of you.

As a teen I pushed on the limits of the gate,
And to drive along with Mom and Dad was first rate,
Then they let me drive alone,
With rules they taught me were to be my own,
I was allowed to test the road,
But not to be squished flat as a toad.

I then left that house and home,
To my own trail to now roam,
I planned my own journey for each day,
After a while sensed Another guiding my way.

I met a special car named Gini and together spent 51
     years,
Now two cars close, occasionally changing gears,
We sped up and down the highways,
Our journey took us on many byways,

We went and did and had so much fun,
All the time realizing there is nothing new under the
      sun.

We spent time together reading the Guide's book,
Even teaching others young and old how to drive and
      look,
We began to see our nothing was something,
Indeed, our own soul was that nothing.

Then one day her car began to slow and stall,
As she continued toward her upward call.
On the backstretch she was failing to keep up the pace,
But said she had a helping Hand and would still finish
      the race,

One day the car simply would not run,
I helped pull her aside and out of the fun and sun,
And soon in that same car in which she was born,
She gently was removed and not even torn,
I am certain her removal did not even hurt.
Now only an empty shell to return to dirt,
We both knew it was only a car on loan,
While on this earth's journey as an alien we did roam.

My car too is no longer my own,
Mine too will run out of gas,
And beside the journey's path,
Will also decay in the grass,
My soul, too, will gently be removed,
As body and rim scatters,
May all see that her and my nothing matters.

                              —Gene Baillie

~

"I had a variety of concerns and exercises about my soul from my childhood; but had two more remarkable seasons of awakening, before I met with that change by which I was brought to those new dispositions, and that new sense of things, that I have since had." A few pages later he writes, "I felt a burning desire to be in everything a complete Christian; and conformed to the blessed image of Christ; and that I might live in all things, according to the pure, sweet and blessed rules of the gospel. I had an eager thirsting after progress in these things; which put me upon pursuing and pressing after them." He then writes of remembering the thoughts of holiness from an earlier time, "My heart panted after this, to lie low before God, as in the dust; that I might be nothing, and that God might be all, that I might become as a little child."

— Jonathan Edwards, Personal Narrative

Our God-given perception of our empty heart and its condition is at the very core of our transformation.

6. Nothing Changes Everything

My wife Gini drew a picture (the one on the cover of this book) on the third-year anniversary of her brain tumor being removed. Although creative, she had never drawn or painted. Gini began to have more trouble with verbal communication and keeping her thoughts together. Drawing became an outlet of communicating that helped her maintain focus on a single subject by way of placing a continuing visual reminder in front of her. As with many of her drawings, this particular picture began simple and evolved. It started out as brown lines that she identified as a lamb. Then she added black and a little yellow. Because she was drawing in watercolor pencils, she was able to wash out the top layer in a couple of places. Watching her, I asked what she had drawn, and she replied, "Nothing." After letting the drawing dry, she wanted to add more and drew a large red heart around the picture that she had called nothing. She then used the water to wash away part of the red color.

To some, this and her other simple drawings might seem insignificant, rudimentary, possibly not worth a place on the fridge. This one, especially, looked strange and washed out, but from my perspective it was a masterpiece depicting a profound picture of a heart with nothing in it—like our human soul.

You see, reader, this life is all about perspective. Our Lord wants us to see everything as He does. Just as my understanding and curiosity of nothing gave my wife's drawing new meaning, I also need further understanding of my own nothing and how to live. Now, I hope to give you a perspective of some of what I saw through this new lens.

Self-esteem: A New View of Self

When I was in high school, I had a great disappointment (but who hasn't?). I always dreamed of being a pro basketball player, a lofty aspiration for a teenager five feet eight inches tall. On a good day, I could only make 20 percent of my shots and 65 percent of my free throws. Being a visionary, accepting limitations has never been my strong point, and I stayed in hot pursuit of stardom.

My senior year I finally graduated from being student manager and made the team. My "big break" began with me sitting on the bench the entire first game. The second game I played for precisely one minute at the end of the game, and the third week, I was replaced by a freshman. This was the first year the state allowed freshmen to play varsity, and this kid was good! I understood quite well why he had taken my place, and finally the reality that I would not make pro became pretty clear to my optimistic mind. The ability necessary to succeed in the basketball world had not been given to me, and my talent tank for basketball was empty, so to speak.

On the other hand, when I was a sophomore, I went out for high school football and was assigned second-string guard. I got to play at the end of the first game when we were already way ahead. In the fourth quarter of our second game of the season, we were ahead by six points when our center hiked the ball over the punter's head and our win disappeared before our eyes, as the other team recovered in the end zone for the final touchdown and extra point.

At practice on Monday, the coach was quite upset with us and had every person center the ball to the punter twenty times. I was the only one who accurately got the ball to him every time. Immediately, I was made first-string center! I look back and recognize God for giving and withholding ability. God adds His planned experiences and qualities specific to each of us. Physical and mental abilities of His choosing are only the start.

Many people live their lives trying to build up their nothingness and make it worth something, just as I tried to make something of my nonexistent basketball ability. They feel that if they are talented or beautiful enough, hardworking or successful enough, rich or selfless enough, then they will finally feel worthy—satisfied with themselves and full of confidence.

> Seeing our nothingness changes our understanding of ourselves. It removes pride, pretentiousness, self-hatred, and despair.

The truth is quite the opposite. Only God is able to make us see exactly who we are and make us feel truly confident at the same time. First, He shows us that we are "nothing of ourselves." Only then can we recognize that Christ is everything—and without Him we have no value (in Him are all things, and in Him we live and move and have our being). On this topic, C. S. Lewis once said, "Non-Christians seem to think that the Incarnation (Jesus becoming a man) implies some particular merit or excellence in humanity. But of course it implies just the reverse: a particular demerit and depravity. No creature that deserved Redemption would need to be redeemed. They that are whole need not the Physician. Christ died for men precisely because men are not worth dying for: To make them worth it."

We are not worth it! We are worthless. We are not whole! We are sinful. We are wasted. We are wasteful. The Law shows us this, but in contrast, the gospel proclaims Jesus lived, died, and rose again to make us worthy, to make us righteous in Him! Only in Him do we have anything, and indeed something is made of our nothing. When the Holy Spirit changes us, our heart is replaced and is now filled with Jesus (our all in all!). Though our old bodies still carry a burden of sin in the midst of our new life, we now have a purpose, and something of infinite value inside of us.

With this transforming knowledge, we no longer have to build our own "sand castles" on sinking sand. We begin to understand that we can stop our endless striving for a sense of worth and belonging. Seeing our nothingness changes our understanding of ourselves. It removes pride, pretentiousness, self-hatred, and despair. Our nothing now has Jesus within, filling it to overflowing. We can go forth, knowing that the Lord will use our nothing for His purposes, for His plan, for our lives, and for others.

As we grow we are also able to find joy in our work and our victories. We can have that joy without pride or fear because we know God is working through us. Just as football practice took my small abilities and made them greater, God takes our ordinary and makes us extraordinary. We are able to do things that even we could not imagine. He changes us constantly during our time on this earth, molding us into all He wants us to be for His purposes and for our good. We dare not taint what God has done by returning to our habit of taking ownership of His gifts. When we forget that all added things are rubbish if we don't have Christ, we can fall into a season of pride in "our" accomplishments or discouragement in the lack of them. God owns and loans attributes and abilities to us for our season on earth. Our work, talent, relationships, calling, body, and personality must be received in full trust and faith, not in ourselves but in God and His will and purpose for our lives. We are only nothing, thankful for what He has given and added to us. "Every good gift and perfect gift is from above, coming down from the Father of lights with whom there is no variation or shadow due to change." So we who are His can rejoice! In choosing to serve God with what He has purchased, each gift cannot, as His possession, be wasted! He has truly made something beautiful out of me, providing my nothing with a part of who He is.

The seeming self-esteem crisis that Americans are facing today (that I believe is a myth and a perceived crisis) could be fixed if only we could go ahead and say, "Yes, I am nothing! In myself, I will never be or have enough!" Then rest in the fact that God is more than we could ever ask or think. By offering, in a sense, our nothing to Him, He opens our eyes to the truth of Romans 11:36: "For from Him and through Him and to Him are all things. To Him be the glory forever! Amen" (NIV). In the realization that we are empty in and of ourselves, God has made us ready to be filled with His Spirit and allows us to share in His glory. Seeing that we are nothing can be the first step to not only finding peace in our new and infinite worth but also knowing we will join in the riches of heaven.

A New View of Trials/Temptations

In my book *The Journey Home*, I spoke of how God often causes our trials to result in blessings. The book is brimming with examples of this truth. For example, the fiercest and most destructive storm also includes the rain that waters the earth producing flowers of every kind. A wild fire devours a landscape but leaves the ashen soil enriched, which then yields a richer crop. He has filled His Word with accounts of diffi-culty and disaster being

> *Seeing that we are nothing can be the first step to not only finding peace in our new and infinite worth but also knowing we will join in the riches of heaven.*

transformed into beauty and grace. The most powerful example is that of the gruesome death of Christ. The world is dark, the followers have scattered, Satan rejoices over his apparent triumph, all hope seems lost. But God, through Jesus dying on the cross and rising from the dead, turned Satan's greatest evil toward mankind into the greatest blessing God the Father could give—eternal life. His children now no longer need to fear death because death was and is swallowed up in victory! Devastation and death are no stumbling block for Jesus. It is simply a canvas on which He can paint His glory.

When you think you have lost everything, and you think you have nothing, remember the God who created is the One who has made something of your nothing! Recall His mercies. You are still here on earth, and if you are thinking to yourself that you have nothing, you obviously still have your God-given mind and body.

When the reality hit that my wife wasn't experiencing only temporary weakness or feeling funny but was now diagnosed with a brain-killing cancer, our worlds were rocked. I was about to lose the wife of my life, the woman whom the Lord used to support, love, and challenge me in all areas of my life. I felt lonely for a while and even experienced some deep discouragement, but I then realized that the Lord was still using both of us for His purposes and all circumstances were still according to His perfect plan. He had been and would continue to be our Lord no matter what.

We have our worldly people relationships and goods for a season—our parents, our children, our jobs, our cars, our health, even our spouses. When God gently pulls back our clinging fingers and takes a loved one home, we truly feel the depth of loss. It is then that we start to understand that the Lord wants us to use our nothingness for His glory and see more clearly He is divesting us of our worldly things, our idols, the desires, and even the people whom we hold most dear. He is declaring that, indeed, He is our one and only Source of life. All things we have and all we do are from, through, and for Him. He is telling us to forsake the broken cisterns and drink from the fountain of life to have our thirst forever quenched.

As for the special woman He placed in my life, Gini also was an ordinary woman made extraordinary by the Lord. I was again reminded of this on my wife's seventieth birthday, that while the outer woman was decaying each day with the slow growth of her brain tumor and the progressive radiation damage, her inner self was being renewed continually as the Lord shone through her smile and every part of her very "being." Some might say that a nearly immobile, nonverbal woman has nothing to offer her own family, let alone the world. As the things of this world grew strangely dim, she indeed was becoming almost nothing! But in actuality, she touched as many people in this condition as she did in her healthiest moments. Because of visits and needed assistance, we had more old and new friends who entered our home than ever before. People were astounded to see my wife's readily apparent cheerfulness, and shortly each realized the trust, peace, and hope we both had in the Lord as we stared into the valley of the shadow of death. *The Journey Home* book I wrote about trials and marriage, as well as discussions on death, led to a myriad of opportunities to share the gospel and turn the glory to God. My wife's often-silent confidence during this time spoke to people as much as her teaching in-depth Bible studies and Sunday school. As Gini shed worldly goods and cares, and became closer to "nothing," her God who is everything was shining much clearer through her.

As we saw the things of this world more dimly, we saw more clearly the things of the Lord put within her. Thus He teaches us peace and trust. She finished well! We watched Philippians 4:4–9 in process!

After a tragedy such as a fire that destroys a home and all belongings, those who have suffered loss will often express, "I have lost everything. I have nothing left." Despite the sadness of losing many things, the person has not lost his life. A few months ago I got a note from missionaries to China. One of their contacts was contemplating belief in Jesus but holding back because he was facing the risk of losing everything and would have nothing left.

> *We learn by experience whether our nothingness has found satisfaction in the* everything *of Christ.*

In both examples, if nothing is something you can "have," then it is actually something. This something is very important. By losing seemingly everything of this life—family, reputation, friends, job, possessions, and safety—and taking hold of Christ, your nothing gains everything. Only when the Spirit of God indwells you, in having your heart of stone removed (see Ezekiel 36:26–27), can you then have a new heart that is truly able to receive from God and be something. Only in pruning can a plant produce more and better fruit (John 15:2 and following). Only in dying in the depths of the earth can a grain of wheat germinate to produce numerous grains of wheat (John 12:24).

Alongside the trials we face in this world are the temptations—those constant pulls that God *allows* us to struggle with, the "something" that the world around us always tries to add to our being. Within your *no-thing* soul, you have a sense of guilt with an inner desire to resist but also the desire to yield to various enticements. These temptations are from Satan. They are tests God *allows* to see how we will handle them and reveal to us whether our faith in God is genuine (God already knows if it is genuine!). We then learn by experience whether our nothingness has found satisfaction in the *everything* of Christ, or if we feel the need to again add rubbish to the pile. As the bait is dangled in front of us, we must remember James 1:17—"Every good and perfect gift is from above, coming down from the Father of the heavenly lights" (NIV).

When we are saved, God provides us with everything needed to add to that nothing that came into the world (2 Peter 1:3). God has given us worth and hope, whereas sin never keeps its promises to quench the thirst of emptiness anyway. With this newfound understanding, I, for one, want good and perfect gifts added to my nothing. I now long for God to remove the things that are not pleasing to Him and are not for my good.

A brief review of the life of Moses might be appropriate as one example of how the Lord uses our lives. During the first forty years of his life, Moses was "saved" by the Lord, and his soul was provided with everything the world could desire; he was in the very palace of the king, treated as if he were the king's son. He then seemingly lost everything, so the next forty years he spent running and in the wilderness. Then God appeared to him in the burning bush as the great "I AM" provider of everything, calling Moses to serve Him, making something of his nothing during the last forty years of his life on this earth.

I know that all things—joyous and painful—bring God glory because He created everything for His own glory! My nothingness in the hands of its Creator is simply journeying on this earthly pathway for His glory. If we meditate on this truth until it is instilled into the core of our earthly lives, then we begin to understand just how God is working through all things (some added to us, some burdening us, and some happening around us). As we then begin to realize that afflictions of any kind are meaningful and are producing in us Christlikeness, we worship! We give praise, honor, and our very nothing to Jesus Christ, who is all we need. Because of what Christ has done for a nothing like me, at every moment of decision my reference point should be "Christ in me, the hope of glory." I will only desire to have Him as my very food and drink, my pure white clothing, and my richest treasure, He who loves me with an everlasting, eternal love. Who else cares for my nothing as Jesus does?

> *For all the sad words of tongue and pen, the saddest are these "It might have been."*
>
> — John Greenleaf Whittier

A New View of Blessings

As a child I helped clean up after a tornado destroyed a family's entire home and all of their possessions. Thinking back to this experience, I am reminded of the record of Job's devastating loss. Almost every year we hear of many who have suffered a similar tragic loss. It is often said of survivors of these and other such tragedies that *they have nothing.* If you think through this phrase, however, you see that nothing is really something. They may have lost all their worldly possessions that humans have termed "everything," but in reality they still have their lives on this earth. Can we label that nothing? But maybe that truly is the answer—they still have their nothing! Now that we understand the word better, we cannot see the term *nothing* to mean loss of all things. In the face of hardship, blessings of God's providence that may have gone unnoticed are now something much more precious. If God has added life, breath, and Christ's value to your nothing soul today, you cannot say you have nothing, no matter what loss you have suffered.

In Revelation 3:17, we learn that one may say, "I have need of nothing" because in Christ we are rich, refined as pure gold. This verse describes people who value their material wealth on earth and do not realize that they are wretched, miserable, poor, blind, and naked. While I believe this is part of the application, in other verses we see that God provides for all our needs in Christ Jesus. Looking at Scripture as a whole, and indeed reading the word *need* before the word *nothing*, we also see the play on words and understand in that sense we have need of this nothing—to be stripped of our wretched, miserable, and worldly lifestyle goals. And we know, as Christians, that we are being refined as gold and are given a heavenly crown, so we are indeed rich as we go to be with the Lord eternally. In 2 Corinthians 6:10, Paul makes an impressive statement. He says he is in a state of "having nothing, yet possessing everything." Just before this passage, 2 Corinthians 4–5 refers to us as jars of clay within our earthly tents and begs that we look forward to heaven through faith in God's promise. While we say our clay vessels and worn tents contain nothing, in and of themselves they are not empty; and we can be assured that when they are filled with the treasure of Christ, anything and everything poured out of our earthly vessel is all of His blessings.

Not only do we have every blessing in the heavenly places, but in Matthew 6:25–26, Christ says He will provide for all the needs of and for our nothing here on earth. These are His words of promise: "Therefore I tell you, do not be anxious about your life, what you will eat or what you will drink, nor about your body, what you will put on. Is not life more than food, and the body more than clothing? Look at the birds of the air: they neither sow nor reap nor gather into barns, and yet your heavenly Father feeds them. Are you not of more value than they?"

Even on our lowest days, we have the promise of His presence and provision and the anticipation of eternity with Him. Because temptations and trials are used to make something of our nothing, we can count even these things as blessings. If surrendered to the Lord, God makes the barren fruitful—and our nothing everything.

A New View of Death

Death. Never has it been so real to me as it is now. In Psalm 39, God says that our human lifetime is like a mere breath, as nothing, before Him. He made us and chose us in Christ before the foundation of the world (Ephesians 1:4). Yet, like a blade of grass, we wither and are no more—we are nothing to the world (in the sense of never having existed).

But remember, nothing in the hands of God is something. I recently read a devotional about how life, our influence, and God's plan continues through us after we die. We do indeed wither like a leaf on a tree, which turns brown, falls to the ground, decays, and gradually becomes indistinguishable. But much like that single leaf, the regenerate child of God also continues to replenish and nourish the next generation of offspring that will appear in the next season. Once we have been made everything in Christ, even in death, our nothing cannot be wasted! Soul and body, I will be kept in heaven, and I know that God made a lasting difference for Himself through my life here on earth.

This influence passed on to our offspring is a part of what is called covenant theology. It is God's stated intention that He is working through the generations. Even something as simple as you reading this book has influenced you in some way, and that will pass through you to your children and grandchildren, even though they may never hear of it or read it. Deuteronomy 7:9, "Know therefore that the LORD your God is God, the faithful God who keeps covenant and steadfast love with those who love Him and keep His commandments, to a thousand generations." Acts 2:39, "For the promise is for you and for your children and for all who are far off, everyone whom the Lord our God calls to Himself."

In this knowledge, I can stand confident when a believing loved one or I face death. To be keenly aware that we are impervious to death's sting is to walk unshaken through the valley of the *shadow of death* because God is with us. I also read of Donald Barnhouse, a Bible teacher from the 1950s, when he lost his wife to cancer while she was only in her thirties. Here is the account.

On the way to the funeral, his oldest daughter looked to her father and asked, "If Jesus died for our sins, why do we still die?"

At that moment, a large truck roared past them. Barnhouse turned to his daughter and asked, "Tell me, sweetheart, would you rather be run over by that truck or its shadow?"

"By the shadow," she replied. "It can't hurt you." Barnhouse nodded and said, "Did you know that the truck of death ran over the Lord Jesus in order that only its shadow might run over us? Your mother has not been overrun by death but by the shadow of death. That is nothing to fear."

Jesus said, "I am the resurrection and the life." Jesus told us, "He who believes in Me, though he may die, he shall live" (John 11:25). Christians hold fast to this promise. That's why everyone who calls Christ their Savior, can say, "O Death, where is your sting? O Hades, where is your victory? The sting of death is sin, and the strength of sin is the law. But thanks be to God, who gives us the victory through our Lord Jesus Christ" (1 Cor. 15:55–57).

Our seeming darkest hour, which should be most fearful, is instead a place filled with the Light of the world! Only the shadow remains because Christ took out the real truck!

It will be a supreme day of rejoicing when I lose my life in death because I will finally shed everything of this worldly life, but my soul will be immediately in the presence of the Lord. And one day on Christ's return, my glorified body will somehow be new and reunited with my soul! First Corinthians 15:41 and following teaches us that our bodies were sown natural bodies and will be raised spiritual bodies. In death, I become nothing to gain everything through Christ as He emptied Himself, came to earth, conquered death, and was raised from the dead as our complete and everlasting Savior, Lord, and Treasure! What a marvelous wonder that we are made in the image of God!

After three and a half short years, C. S. Lewis lost his beloved wife Joy to cancer. In his book *A Grief Observed*, he writes about his thoughts and experiences with death in this situation: "God has not been trying an experiment on my faith or love in order to find out their quality. He knew it already. It was I who didn't. In this trial He makes us occupy the dock, the witness box, and the bench all at once. He always knew that my temple was a house of cards. His only way of making me realize the fact was to knock it down."

At death, we cannot keep or add even a minute, a thing, an idea, or whatever to the nothing we brought into this world. We emphatically leave this life with not anything added of ourselves. But thanks be to God that, as a Christian, our nothing is clothed with the righteousness of Christ and His communicable attributes. This process of being adopted by God into His family miraculously adds something to us that was not only absent but was impossible without Him.

So, now I take the nothing I brought into the world and through the provision of God use all He provides for His glory while on earth as an alien and stranger. I can now face death with courage because Christ in me is the hope of glory, and I will have eternal life with Him forever as my nothing is taken out of this world.

"Communicable Attributes." These are the attributes that God has chosen to share with mankind. In his *Systematic Theology* text, Wayne Grudem asks, "How is God like us in his being, and in mental and moral attributes?" (1994, 185–225). He then explains that communicable attributes are the attributes of God that are more shared with us than the incommunicable attributes. This is not an absolute division but simply a way to organize and present them. Some of these communicable attributes of which we have only a part of the whole of that attribute of God are: knowledge, faithfulness, goodness, love, mercy, grace, patience, and peace.

Personal Note

We have an annual beach week with family, and as is tradition, we spend some time digging in the sand, making lopsided sand castles and shallow moats. No matter how tightly we pack the sand or how perfect the handmade structures are, the wind and the tide constantly destroy all evidence of our careful handi-work. In the face of everyday abrasion and washing, these sand castles quickly return to their original state of being nothing but sand. Our souls are the same.

If we spend all our earthly life trying to build our nothing into significance—building towers of power, self-glory, wealth, popularity, and possessions—it will all be for naught. When we die, it will all be washed away in the face of God's holiness, and we are left with only the nothing that we are (Luke 12:19–21).

But if the Holy Spirit changes our heart and it belongs to Christ, He becomes our valuable treasure. We see that building with our sand is useless, and we begin to build firmly based on the Rock of His Word and righteousness He has given us, knowing we have now been made living stones (1 Peter 2:4–12). We are stripped bare, much as Christ was. Our false dignities are gone, and now we desire that our nothing soul should be covered, clothed, and built up by and in Christ.

Knowing that I am nothing has changed my life and given me eyes to see my high calling to live all for Christ's glory. It removes my need to fret over being worthy of love and acceptance and gives me comfort in and under the weight of great trials—even death. It shows me that Christ is free to make of, in, and through me something more than a wasted life, and assures me that everything—pain, sorrow, joy, failings, successes, mistakes, obedience—will be used for my good and to bring Him glory. It truly is my greatest accomplishment with my God-given nothing.

~

I'd rather have Jesus
Than all the silver and all of the gold, oh
I'd rather have Jesus
Than all of the riches and wealth untold, oh
I'd rather have Jesus
Than all of the houses and all of the land
I'd rather have Jesus
More than anything

— Rhea F. Miller, 1922

~

Although an engagement ring has promises or
memories, is pretty, and even clings tightly to
its worldly, expensive, and glittering diamond,
it is empty unless it is filled with a finger of
a living soul, then it becomes something
significant.

~

All I have needed Thy hand hath provided;
Great is Thy faithfulness, Lord, unto me!
— Thomas O. Chisholm, 1923

~

This I recall to my mind,
Therefore I have hope.
Through the Lord's mercies we are not consumed,
Because His compassions fail not.
They are new every morning;
Great is Your faithfulness.
"The Lord is my portion," says my soul,
"Therefore I hope in Him!"
— Lamentations 3:21-24 NKJV

~

You contribute nothing to your salvation except the sin that made it necessary. . . . I assert that nothing ever comes to pass without a cause. . . . From love arises hatred of those things which are contrary to what we love, or which oppose and thwart us in those things that we delight in.
—Jonathan Edwards, "Miscellanys," 1723

~

"You always get yourself in a fret over nothing."
— Auntie Em
"If I only had a brain. . . . I would not be just a nuffin', my head all full of stuffin'."
— Scarecrow, *The Wizard of Oz*

For nine months before my wife Gini died of her brain cancer, she could no longer talk. But it was amazing what she could "say" without saying a word. Her eyes, her smile, her nod of the head. We might say she was saying nothing, but indeed she was communicating very clearly.

7. Don't Waste Your Nothing

Francis Schaeffer describes nothing nothing as "We are considering existence, the fact that something is there. Remember Jean-Paul Sartre's statement that the basic philosophic question is that something is there rather than nothing being there. The first basic answer is that everything that exists has come out of absolutely nothing. In other words, you begin with nothing. Now, to hold this view, it must be absolutely nothing. It must be what I call nothing nothing. It cannot be nothing something or something nothing. If one is to accept this answer, it must be nothing nothing, which means there must be no energy, no mass, no motion, and no personality" (*He Is There and He Is Not Silent*, 1972).

So what have you learned? Nothing! You have learned that nothing is necessary, nothing is significant in language and creation, nothing is used throughout Scripture, and nothing is possibly the empty human soul. I have shared with you how the transforming power of understanding nothing has changed my perspective as a Christian.

But what about you? How are you to apply this? Whether or not you and I fully understand nothing is not the point. God has provided His light to shine in the darkness and in the emptiness of our hearts that we might serve Him with all our might. Any understanding of truth has been given to us because God wants us to be fully engaged with Him and for His kingdom. This message is for everyone in every phase of life.

If you're struggling with applying this concept of nothingness to your life, come like the writer of "Rock of Ages" crying,

> Nothing in my hands I bring,
> Simply to the cross I cling.
> Naked come to thee for dress,
> Helpless come to thee for grace,
> Foul I to the fountain fly,
> Help me Savior or I die.

> —Augustus Toplady, 1763

Admit two things: First, who you are and what you have is only nothing apart from what God has added, and second, only God can make something from nothing (both from absolutely no thing at all and also from your something nothing). This realization is the beginning of something wonderful. God transforms and completely changes souls and uses them for His glory. Once He has changed you, your *nothing* is then a new *something* unique and special to God because He uses *everything* for His glory and your good. Remember Christ's account of the boy with five loaves and two fish. The meager lunch seemed next to nothing in comparison to the size of the crowd, but when offered up to Jesus that basket of nothingness overflowed and became more than enough.

As a Christian you, too, can be used that way. God has redeemed your nothing soul and given you added attributes and abilities to glorify Him to overflowing in every aspect of your life. You are the Lord's chosen; you are special in His sight and useful as a vessel molded for His use. You alone have hands to play your music to Him. You alone have a voice to sing your praises to Him. You alone have ears to hear and understand His Word as He enables you. You alone have a voice with which to proclaim His truth.

If you are young, don't forget that what you choose to do today with your nothing and God-given additions is important. In each day there are 86,400 moments we call seconds. Seek not to simply "live in the moment" but recognize that every and all moments make up a lifetime, built up in Christ or to selfishly serve yourself. Likewise, if you are a young mom, you may be thinking of the seeming nothing-ness along with feeling that your work in the home is insignificant. But, God has added to your nothing the ability to be a critical instrument during your child's early life—possibly the most crucial part. Entrust your soul to God's purpose, and you will bring Him glory in raising children, as well as being an example of a loving, respecting wife. God directs you to follow His example of love and care, and your life is not wasted. A retiree, like myself, may struggle with feeling that he or she has little important left to offer the world, but know that the God who makes something of nothing has care over that soul too. Wake up each day knowing that there is a plan and purpose in each moment of every day. Whether confined or while reaching out to support others whenever possible, we can still give God glory by refusing self-centeredness and by worshipping Christ through word and prayer.

When life's journey takes a turn that strips you of some of your added things through trial, affliction, suffering, or a period of waiting, do not be discour-aged. Even when you feel that you are of little use and accomplishing nothing, remember, if you can accom-plish nothing, it must be something! God uses every phase of our lives when we are His.

Look at the people of the Bible. Abraham and Sarah were childless, Joseph imprisoned, Gideon a coward, Mary a teenage girl, Matthew a tax collector, Peter a fisherman, Paul a murderous zealot. It is the ordinary, poor, barren, broken people whom God chooses and then provides with everything and directs their lives, for His glory. So, put your trust in Him.

I personally can assure you that, while you may feel that you are worthless—or becoming worth *less*— the God who provided your added gifts and guided your every step previously will do it again. You may or may not see that even something such as my fading wife's abilities but also her trust, rest, and peace in painful circumstances are what He had added. She still smiled, and people visiting or seeing her in a wheelchair readily saw trust and peace in her eyes, even though she could not speak a word. These things testify loudly of Him to the world, bringing Him immense glory. Take comfort! Not an ounce of your life will be wasted in His hands. Each moment has a thread of purpose strung through it. Pursue trust in Christ, and you need not fear uselessness.

> Even when you feel that you are of little use and accomplishing nothing, remember, . . . God uses every phase of our lives when we are His.

In what phase of life do you find yourself? What are you doing with your nothing? By God's grace He has made you something! How do you plan not to waste *your* nothing? Here is your challenge: no matter who you are or where you are, take the parts of your day or the current season of your life that you might define as nothing or meaningless. Submit those feelings to the Word of God, which encourages us to see those times as an opportunity to glorify God in our hearts and minds. Doing laundry, driving to and from work, waiting for marriage, pumping gas, paying the bills, and other mundane tasks or seasons still have the purpose of proclaiming the excellences of Him who called us out of darkness into marvelous light.

If you are an agnostic or an atheist, you may feel and believe life is meaningless. Does this thought not unnerve you? Though the difference in our beliefs may be night and day, here is one thing on which we can agree. Eventually you will move from this life to the next, and all of the things that you strove to add to your nothing-soul will have no lasting value and, therefore, no ultimate meaning—in other words, meaningless! What can be said for the Christ-less soul? When Ephesians 1:10 comes to pass and His "plan for the fullness of time, to unite all things in Him, things in heaven and things on earth" is complete, you will be absent the Mediator, Jesus Christ, subject to God's wrath forever. All of your earthly treasures and accomplishments will be for naught. He does not need any of us but chooses to redeem us. So, I plead with you to ask the Lord to provide His something for your nothing while on this earth. Reflect His light, testify to what He has done, engage in business for Him. Rejoice. Share His blessings. Experience the beauty of Job 33:29–30:

> *God does not need any of us but chooses to redeem us.*

Behold, God does all these things,
    twice, three times, with a man,
to bring back his soul from the pit,
    that he may be lighted with the light of life.

In John 3:30, John the Baptist says, "He must increase, but I must decrease" (NASB). When you recognize that you are simply nothing, an empty soul, then you can be filled up with all that Christ is. Suddenly, your nothing is made something of eternal value and purpose toward the kingdom of God. Christ says in Matthew 16:25–26, "For whoever wishes to save his life will lose it; but whoever loses his life for My sake will find it. For what will it profit a man if he gains the whole world and forfeits his soul? Or what will a man give in exchange for his soul?" (NASB).

If we seek to preserve our lives by adding to our souls through our own means—planning, riches, relationships, success, self-righteousness—we will have no effect on bringing any eternal significance to the nothing we came into the world with. Only by losing our lives, surrendering them wholly to the purpose and molding of our Creator God, will we make of them anything of worth.

You are nothing without Christ's transferred righteousness and His direction. If you have and are nothing without God but gain everything with Him, you have to ask, "What do I lose?" Nothing. In the fullest sense, you do not have anything to lose in surrendering yourself to Him. "Seek first the kingdom of God, and His righteousness, and all these things will be added unto you." So for the glory of Christ and the gain of your soul, choose today to place your nothing in His hands. I assure you, it will not be wasted.

~

The Prayer of a Nothing-Soul

Lord Jesus,

As I consider my life and inevitable death, I pray that You will use my earthly journey mightily. Lord, I purpose here and now to finish well.

I was created out of nothing at all, and I was nothing before I came to know You. But God, You gave me knowledge and the ability to call upon Your name. You have given me Your righteousness, Your spotless record, and made my soul something of value. Help me not to waste this nothing that You have now made something! Lord, help me to live out this earthly life to serve You all my days in the newness of life that You provided. Let me not exist for myself but for You and to tell others about Your saving grace and mercy.

I can rest and trust, Jesus, because I know that You will take care of me and will not allow testing or temptations beyond what You have given me strength, courage, and peace to bear (1 Corinthians 10:13). You are refining me in the furnace of affliction for Your glory. Prepare me for the death of this body You provided. Let me leave this world with my nothing resting completely in the unshakable truth that Christ died for me, willingly suffering as a part of Your perfect plan, so that I may know that death will not have victory. Death only provides that passage of a closer walk with You because I enter into Your presence forever.

Lord Jesus, I fail miserably every day, but help me to continually come back to knowing "nothing" except You crucified. O great Conductor, orchestrate my nothingness with the rest of Your creation that my life might make beautiful music for You. I do not want to be a wasted noisy gong or a clanging cymbal! Help me to understand and properly use my nothing to the praise of Your grace. I thank You for all that You have added to me. To You, Christ Jesus, be the glory!

~

For you formed my inward parts;
  you knitted me together in my mother's womb.
I praise you, for I am fearfully and wonderfully made.
Wonderful are your works;
  my soul knows it very well.
My frame was not hidden from you
when I was being made in secret,
  intricately woven in the depths of the earth.
Your eyes saw my unformed substance;
in your book were written, every one of them,
  the days that were formed for me,
  when as yet there was none of them.

— Psalm 139:13–16

~

He restores my soul.
He leads me in paths of righteousness . . . .

— Psalm 23:3

The soul is very real—the difference between life and a dead body.

8. *Nothing Is for Real!*

My wife Gini had twenty-two songs for us to choose from to sing at her funeral. I will list the title or first lines as they tell much of her heart and message she wanted to pass on.

Jesus, Lover of My Soul
In Christ Alone
How Deep the Father's Love for Us
Before the Throne of God Above
Arise, My Soul, Arise
May All Who Come Behind Find Us Faithful
Amazing Grace
You Are My All in All
Amazing Love
Come Thou Fount of Many Blessings
O Love That Will Not Let Me Go
Be Thou My Vision

When You Pass through the Waters, I Will Be
    with You
May the Mind of Christ, My Savior
Blessed Be Your Name
What a Friend We Have in Jesus
Great Is Thy Faithfulness
How Great Thou Art
A Mighty Fortress Is Our God
Holy, Holy, Holy
Lord, Let Me Never Outlive My Love for Thee
A Christian Home

Gini Baillie, the wife of my life for fifty-one and a half years, departed this world on May 21, 2015. I witnessed the departure of her soul from her body as she took her last breath and then confirmed this fact when I viewed her body at the funeral home in preparation for visitation. There was still a body that we could identify as hers, but it was apparent that it was lifeless. I have no problem in using the word *it* because the Gini we knew was no longer a living being on earth. I knew that her cancer-ridden brain was still in that body but no longer functioning. I know that we have pictures and memories that are "living" on. I know that her legacy to all of her biological and foster children as well as her many spiritual children will continue.

As with all of us, Gini was always on a path moving toward a goal on her journey. But which path we are on is important. She sought the least worldly and most God-glorifying path as she asked the Lord's guidance for the steps she took. Her desire was to serve Him all her days and finish well. She liked my life verse: "In his mind or heart, man plans his way, but the Lord guides and directs each step" (Proverbs 16:9 author's paraphrase). But she favored her life verse even more: "I have no greater joy than to hear that my children [and grandchildren] are walking in the truth" (3 John 4). She desired to walk the correct God-ordained-and-directed path so that those who followed her might do the same. Her favorite song was modified to be personal: "May all who come behind me find me faithful."

Gini's soul had departed her body, that part of her being that throughout this book I have attempted to describe to you as "nothing" or the "no man" part of our being. I know for certain that this nothing of hers is really something and is absent from the body but present with the Lord. That soul will be given a new body. I was actually able to witness firsthand what our soul means to our earthly body during the season of our lifetime on earth—the miracle of God's creative powers with dust, water, and air, as described in Psalm 139:14 with these words: "I am fearfully and wonderfully made, . . . my soul knows it"!

Many of us are scared of death, but if you are a Christian, there is no need or reason to be frightened. We have read and been taught the truth from the Bible that death has lost its sting because of the death and resurrection of Jesus Christ; but we are still scared, not satisfied with the answers and teaching we hear until we have rest, peace, and trust in the hope given to us.

As we get older or as we go through trials, we begin to understand more clearly, but one of the best ways to be certain is to be beside someone when they die. Some have pain, and all suffer in some way. But, if we know Jesus and truly rest and trust in Him, having faith provided to us (with its resultant hope), then He will not give us more than we can bear and will hold our hand throughout the journey!

The "worst" ending for Christians is to be immediately in the presence of the Lord when we die, resurrected and more alive than we have ever been! For you see, I watched my wife walk through the valley of the shadow of death without fear and in complete trust and rest in Jesus. I know all the more certainly that it was only a shadow! I could not clearly see as she could, but I could hold her hand until Jesus only was holding her hand for that last step. But, I knew and am understanding only in part the unveiling of His glory as she was stripped of the worldly. I saw the realization and truth of 1 Corinthians 13:12—"For now we see in a mirror dimly, but then face to face. Now I know in part; then I shall know fully, even as I have been fully known."

Nancy Guthrie edited *O Love That Will Not Let Me Go*, a collection of meditations drawn from the sermons and writings of pastors and theologians. In a chapter entitled "Sickness: The Soul's Undressing," she includes Jeremy Taylor's comments written in the 1600s. The opening paragraph is

In sickness the soul begins to dress herself for
immortality. First, she unties the strings of
vanity that made her upper garment cleave to
the world and sit uneasy; she puts off the light
and fantastic summer robe of lust and wanton
appetite; and as soon as that lascivious girdle
is thrown away, . . . then that which called us
formerly to serve the manliness of the body, and
the childishness of the soul, keeps us waking,
to divide the hours with . . . prayer and groans.
Then the flesh sets uneasily and dwells in
sorrow. The spirit feels itself at ease, freed from
the petulant solicitations of those passions which
in health were as busy and restless as atoms in
the sun, always dancing, and always busy, and
never sitting down, till a sad night of grief and
uneasiness draws the veil, and lets them die
alone in secret dishonor. Next to this, the soul,
by the help of sickness, knocks off the fetters of
pride and vainer complacencies. Then she draws
the curtains, and stops the light from coming
in, and takes the pictures down, those fantastic
images of self-love and gay remembrances of
vain opinion and popular noises.

To the several pages of description that follow, I
have also added and intermixed my own observations. There continues the progressive stripping of
layers of worldly philosophy, wisdom, wit, possessions,
animosities, discourse, pride veiled as humility, anger,
and so much more. When sickness and suffering lasts

for a long time, and there is a deadly diagnosis as in the case of my wife, there is also the need to be stripped of the accolades and hearing your eulogy spoken before your funeral! As the stripping occurs, we see faith demonstrating itself to be a powerful and mighty grace at the approach of death, accompanied by a peace that is beyond understanding. For, in our days of health it is easy to put trust in God for His loving care and even His provided escape from the bounds of a trial. But, as we approach the edge of our grave, then we truly see our faith and hope so much closer to the promised reality of eternal life. So, God is dressing us for heaven by the undressing and removal of all but the soul. He must have us struggle, resist the devil, contest the weakness of nature, and against hope believe in hope, thus resigning ourselves completely to God's sovereign will, knowing He chose us, knowing too that dying is the realization of His promises, that we will be more alive than we have ever been! A quiet grave remains, a legacy remains for a season, the pleasant lot into which we were placed is now void of our literal and bodily presence, but our soul is then at perfect peace with the Lord, enjoying and praising Him eternally.

Again, for the Christian, the labor process of the gradual stripping away of the worldly is not guaranteed

> *God is dressing us for heaven by the undressing and removal of all but the soul.*

to be easy or short—medicines or various treatments may or may not be required—but the actual delivery is always instantaneous. My own wife's journey was four years long after her diagnosis of the deadly brain cancer called glioblastoma. Although the journey was largely peaceful, she did have intermittent difficult steps as I held her hand. These included blood clots in her lungs, disorientation, bone marrow failure, seizures, a broken hip, and pneumonia. But she was at rest and peace in her Jesus who was able to meet her every need. Jesus also provided for her loving care, which included His enabling me. Her death was a beautiful process, and although it was not fun, sitting at her bedside in our home, holding her hand, was a time of joy and rejoicing that our Lord was finished with her work on this earth. Everything was for her good and the good of all of those who came in contact with her, and was for His glory. We all are sent to death to secure eternal life.

But, not so for the unbeliever. I cannot imagine or describe what happens to his soul, but I am certain it is a place of no joy, no hope, and unending sorrow and torment. I also know that without love for and faith in the Lord, no hope exists.

We humans also love our sin, and we know the wages of sin is death. If we remain wrapped up in our own small package, without the God-given gift of saving faith, then we will not gain His reward. Like Lazarus we must have our death clothes stripped away. Faith comes as that free gift but demands changes.

We cannot stay in our sinful environment, but instead we desire to progress on our journey's path toward Christ and His work for us to do. Then the wages received is guaranteed eternal life! Walk in the footsteps of the faith the Lord gives and live.

Each morning I read some of the Bible to Gini, and at night family members with Gini said the Twenty-third Psalm before singing our song about grace and peace. What peace I observed growing within Gini as we read not only this psalm but her extensive list of memorized passages. And the same was true of myself. In Psalm 23, one verse became increasingly important to me as I experienced the changes in both my wife and myself. Verse 3 says, "He restores my soul. He leads me in paths of righteousness." As I reflect, I became more and more aware of how God truly restores our souls. There was a process of stripping of the worldly that occurred in Gini. The things of earth became progressively more dim and unimportant. She closed her eyes often but always was listening. The best balm for the ears are words of comfort!

But, I also want to now tell you that the same was and is occurring in me, just in an earlier stage. I know we were going through this process together all of our married years. As we both became older, we began to realize more clearly the things of earth were not the most important anymore; however, we were still holding the worldly very tightly. Now, within myself, I can see how the Lord has begun to strip away the layers of my own worldly life. He is stripping, and as my body, too, will take its last breath, my soul also will be absent from the body as "no one" or "no man," restored to my Creator, God Himself. My body, without its soul, can then be referred to as "it" and "nothing," in the sense of "not anything at all."

Now, we come full circle to the beginning of this book, to see the two ways we understand the concept of nothing. One is our common but often misapplied usage of "not anything at all"; the other is the very core of our being while alive on this

> *Even though I walk through the valley of the shadow of death, I will fear no evil, for you are with me; your rod and your staff, they comfort me.*
>
> — Psalm 23:4

earth, the "no one" or "no man" part that makes our body something! That body is useful to the Lord while He has us on this earth, then He returns the empty shell to the earth. For the Christian, He takes our soul to be with Him in eternity. At that moment, He not only perfects and completes us but promises to give our soul a new body.

He is leading me in paths of righteousness. He is restoring my soul as He does with all His children, preparing me for departing this world also. I also see the beginnings of the fading of any fear of death and the rising peace, trust, and rest within my very being. Gini was a little ahead of me on this journey, and I perceive the end of my journey is only a little up the path, just beyond the next bend.

My legacy doesn't matter. It isn't important that I be remembered. It's important that when I stand before the Lord, He says, "Well done, good and faithful servant." I want to finish strong.

— James Dobson

I have fought the good fight, I have finished the race, I have kept the faith.

— 2 Timothy 4:7

And I am sure of this, that he who began a good work in you will bring it to completion at the day of Jesus Christ.

— Philippians 1:6

So as to walk in a manner worthy of the Lord, fully pleasing to him, bearing fruit in every good work and increasing in the knowledge of God. May you be strengthened with all power, according to his glorious might, for all endurance and patience with joy, giving thanks to the Father, who has qualified you to share in the inheritance of the saints in light. He has delivered us from the domain of darkness and transferred us to the kingdom of his beloved Son, in whom we have redemption, the forgiveness of sins.

— Colossians 1:10–14

May you hear, "Well done, good and faithful servant. You have been faithful over a little; I will set you over much. Enter into the joy of your Master."

9. Finishing Well

As you read this last chapter title, you may have wondered why this topic is in a book about nothing, or you may have immediately thought of some illustrations of ways you consider finishing this life well. Or to continue the double-meaning theme, finishing well has nothing in common with the rest of this book.

Let's start with some biblical illustrations that include the passage from Philippians 3:13–14, "But one thing I do: forgetting what lies behind and straining forward to what lies ahead, I press on toward the goal for the prize of the upward call of God in Christ Jesus." The entire chapter further explains "pressing on" toward the goal. Consider 1 Corinthians 9:24–25 about an athlete running a race and Hebrews 12:1-2 about running with endurance the race that is set before us. Our mental image is that of someone running his hardest and crossing the finish line, breaking the tape with a flourish and resounding crowd applause!

Still, what about the person who cannot run or even walk, who has to be fed and needs to be pushed in a wheelchair everywhere? The person who has radiation dementia or terminal cancer and cannot talk, teach, or discuss as in former days but is still on this earth doing what God desires and according to His plan? It seems as if this person is not doing anything. We sometimes wonder at someone we see who is suffering and ask why. She may express, "What am I supposed to be doing?" "I cannot finish." "There is no one to help me." "I am alone and cannot take the next step." "I cannot do anything." You may be reading this and be that someone! You feel as though you have nothing left. That is not true! You may be on the backstretch of your race and cannot yet see the finish line, but you do still have your nothing (that is something) left. You may be at a walk or crawl or even stopped, but you are "still in the race"! With the Lord's help, you will be able to finish, often with the help of others. No one seems to be visiting you, but then a caregiver is required. That is a person brought into your life seeming to serve, but the Lord has a purpose in that person's life and walk also as you strain forward together toward the finish line.

Let me share a couple of things as you realize that those who finish the race of life on this earth rarely have even a small cheering crowd to witness their crossing the finish line. Many, including quite a few in the Bible, did not finish well. So many others in

Scripture stumbled or failed for a time on the back-stretch, but the Lord provided for them to finish well. Hebrews 11 is a chapter of only some of those recorded as examples for us. What follows is Hebrews 12:1–2, "Therefore, since we are surrounded by so great a cloud of witnesses, let us also lay aside every weight, and the sin which clings so closely, and let us run with endurance the race that is set before us, looking to Jesus, the

> *You may be on the backstretch of your race and cannot yet see the finish line, but you do still have your nothing (that is something) left.*

founder and perfecter of our faith." Even though our last days on this earth are often nearly alone and not that image of a fast runner, a great cloud of witnesses is in heaven and somehow rejoicing at our finish. It is not the end, only the finish of our earthly life!

I remember going to one of my son-in-law's Boston Marathon races where he finished in the top 10 percent. Besides being so proud to see him finish well, I was also impressed by the dad who pushed his son with cerebral palsy across the finish line. That son could not run, could not talk, and had to be placed in a modified wheelchair, but he "ran" and finished the race the same as the many others—and this Team Hoyt ran it thirty years! You can be about the plan of God both in active and passive ways.

Let us now consider Jesus Himself. During His three years of ministry on this earth, He was most visible in His teaching, admonishing, healing the sick and blind, casting out demons, and performing all kinds of miracles. Some were done in a seemingly passive or invisible way, like healing the centurion's son (Matthew 8:5–13). He finished well by hanging on a cross, seeming to be doing nothing but dying, even saying, "It is finished." But that ministry was a spectacular, suffering, and crowning finish as part of His Father's plan and purpose. Do you see those words I used? Spectacular in the sense that He was made a spectacle and scorned, treated as a nobody, suffered the cruelest of inhumane deaths, but then rose from the dead as a crowning event worthy of the King of heaven that He is!

Each of our lives has many phases we might consider more active or more passive. I was a pathologist who helped make diagnoses from parts of our bodies that were taken out to examine under the microscope, as well as blood samples for testing that often revealed what was wrong, with subsequent suggestions for treatments. I was a consultant pathologist for the last moon mission and for SkyLab. I taught pathologists here and in Australia, became president of the national society with all those accolades and much more that were important to me but less important to family. When my wife developed her brain cancer, I retired to care for her in our home. Like Paul, all of my listed worldly accomplishments were not as important as my relationship with Christ. But, wait, now I also was no longer teaching inductive Bible studies or having weekly accountability studies for people reading through the Bible. This backstretch leg of our race was certainly much different. At the time, both Gini and I were still following His plan but seeing it as more passive. Although fewer in number than initially, people came to our home for mutual counsel and encouragement, to pray together, and to discuss the process of going through difficult times with the Lord's help.

There was also the time to write a book that I never thought possible. My prayer is that this and the companion book *The Journey Home* will encourage many and be used for His glory and His alone. I, too, am on my journey home. My nothing will depart this earth; I will have no breath or heartbeat, no talking or walking, no working or serving, no reading or even blinking, no accolades or earthly possessions in hand. But while I am here, I am going to endeavor to do all things as unto the Lord (Colossians 3:23–24). I am thankful for the abilities He has given me for this season that include sight with the ability to read, to each day better understand His Word and His plan for my life.

Back to my earlier description of the person who no longer is that sharp, fit, and fast runner. That description fits many of us and even those you know, but it is the exact description of the wife of my life. She no longer did things for the Lord the way she had before her brain cancer was discovered in 2011. No more teaching kids and adults the truth of God's Word with puppets and stories or weighty inductive studies. No more teaching and helping her own children and grandchildren to cook or to invite others into our home or to meet numerous needs. And all with wit and humor! The list could go on for many pages. Those who entered our house saw her in her wheelchair, noticed her ready and captivating smile, heard her sing, and became interested in what occurred. They were brought into the story of a woman who seemed to be doing very little, almost nothing—but still did everything the Lord planned for her. Instead of asking what good was coming from watching and waiting for her to die, we instead saw that the Lord has eternal benefits beyond what we can think or see. Gini finished well by understanding that any affliction and suffering has many purposes in the plan of our sovereign God, and one is impacting the lives of others who are traveling on this journey with us for moments to years! My listing the personal aspects of our lives is not important except to bring you into the story of Jesus as the "I AM" to provide for all of your needs, and the One to rest and trust in now and throughout eternity. Both His life and death provided for our salvation— and the hope of eternal life with Him.

As you rest and trust in Him, He will guard your heart and hold your hand . . . for that last step across the finish line!

Paul in Philippians 3 comments on all the present things in his life that could be reasons for his confidence but says whatever gain he had he counts as loss compared to knowing Christ. In an earlier chapter, I mentioned a verse from this passage where Paul suffered the loss of all things but considered them as rubbish (Philippians 3:4–11). All of the things that we have been discussing concerning ourselves are often in the past tense. It is easy to get depressed and even angry as the things of earth and your abilities begin to fade; however, instead look not to the past but to the present and the goal that is in front of you—that finish line—leaving the manner of the now-slow pace of your run, as well as the day that you cross that finish line, in God's hands. He is leading us step by step and has a perfect plan in place.

Look again at the verse from Philippians 3:13 where you are told to forget what lies behind and strain forward. You are to count it all joy when you encounter various trials and obstacles on your journey (James 1:2). As hymn writer Helen Lemmel suggests, turn your eyes upon Jesus and know that the things of earth are growing strangely dim in the light of His glory and grace. You are to rejoice always, each and every day, at what the Lord is doing. He will grant you a peace that is way beyond your understanding. As you rest and trust in Him, He will guard your heart and hold your hand, as He held ours, for that last step across the finish line! (See Philippians 4:4–9.)

As I pushed my wife in the wheelchair for a "walk" on a sunny day, fed her, took her to the bathroom, transferred her, put on her lipstick—our conversation being an occasional nod of the head—or helped with any number of things she no longer did for herself, we easily could have said, "Why me? Why this seeming uselessness?" Instead, I plead with you that you are still enjoying God's favor and are part of His perfect plan for your life. Continue to strive to "run" the race He has set before you for the number of days He has for you! Or, another example I have used is that of a straight arrow. The Lord is preparing us in a similar way an arrow is made and used. First, the right part of a tree is selected, then the bark is removed and initial cuts are made to remove knots and other imperfections. Then drying and again cutting to make sure all is straight and true, followed by careful, progressive, and fine sanding. Finally it is completed with an arrowhead and notch, then placed in the quiver to do "nothing" until selected and shot to a predetermined place for a predetermined purpose. Praise Him and give Him the glory and, as you rest and trust in Him, know that you will finish well.

Whatever affliction and suffering you or a loved one are currently going through, trust Him and His plan. If you have not yet had "significant" difficulties or trials, I pray you, too, will take comfort in knowing that God is directing each step you take within His perfect plan. Finish well, my friend.

~

Appendix: Thinking More about Nothing

Not yet full of *nothing*? Do you still feel empty and want something more? The following are a few of the myriad of loose notes I have compiled that touch on some new ideas or expand on some of the existing ideas of *nothing* and similar words that express the "not anything" concept.

I want to arouse your interest in nothing and additional similar words used for the concept of nothing and then delve deeper into the concept. Similar to a roller-coaster ride, I want that interest to rise quite steeply to the point of stillness and contemplation so that, seeming to be at that point of nothingness, you then accelerate on a learning curve that begins to quickly move to greater understanding and application!

Who are you, where did you come from, what is your purpose on this earth, and where will you spend eternity? When we think of nothing, I suggest we have to consider a dual concept: the usual meaning we default to, as well as a deep core and soul meaning I have suggested. We sometimes think of our "core being" as our heart as well. Although I introduced a few words in Scripture that have similar meaning and concept with the nothing concept that was foremost, I have purposely made this book short. But now I encourage you to see how the Lord directs your path and steps on your journey as an alien and stranger on this earth—that you might see more clearly the Lord's leading hand as He holds yours, for every step you take.

John 15:5 says, "I am the vine; you are the branches. Whoever abides in me and I in him, he it is that bears much fruit, for apart from me you can do nothing." Is this a different sense of nothing than what you usually think? If you are separated from Christ, you are still living your life on this earth, but it is not for His fruit bearing; it is for your own. You are doing nothing with your life that is God centered, but you are still doing! So, you can still do nothing; it is just not connected to Christ, and the end result is a wasted nothing.

In the presented chapters, I have not wanted to stray down too many rabbit trails and lose our mutual goal (and hopefully the Lord's) in directing your thoughts. I am praying that you might now see the many corollary aspects of life with the corresponding Scriptures and words that would take you to greater heights of knowledge and understanding. My hope is that you might further study and contemplate God's revealed truth and wisdom for your life so that you do not waste your nothing.

For starters, think of the many worship songs and hymns you have sung or listened to that include ideas such as opening the eyes of your heart, seeing Him as your all in all, giving your all to Him. Lyrics about how your soul thirsts for the living God and you give your heart to Him. Musical pleas of "Holy Spirit, mold me, fill me, change me; give to me Your righteousness." And other declarations: "I am empty, and You are all my heart is living for; take my life, and let it be consecrated, Lord, to Thee."

Now consider additional Scripture passages and words that help us see that God changes hearts, putting His Spirit within our very souls, making us a new creation that is clothed differently and capable of giving Him praise and honor with His gift of salvation and righteousness.

Philippians 3:7–9

But whatever gain I had, I counted as loss for the sake of Christ. Indeed, I count everything as loss because of the surpassing worth of knowing Christ Jesus my Lord. For His sake I have suffered the loss of all things and count them as rubbish, in order that I may gain Christ and be found in Him, not having a righteousness of my own that comes from the law, but that which comes through faith in Christ, the righteousness from God that depends on faith.

Let us look again in a little more depth at this passage that incorporates some additional thoughts. As we have previously noted, all the words in Greek are extremely important to our understanding and application, but in verses 7 and 8, the word for *loss* is a Greek word meaning "to regard a thing as loss." I think this is in the realm of losing everything (consider in the sense of whatever we have added for this earthly life) so that we are left with nothing. Because some theologians point out this loss follows the words "whatever gain" and is a loss of things that we formerly valued, there has been a change! Contrary to Paul, we often see gain, then loss causes us great pain!

Also quite important to the understanding of these verses is the Greek of the translated word *count*, having the aspects of "account, consider, deem, think" but also the context in other passages meaning "go before, lead, rule, command, and have authority over." In verse 9 we are "found in Him." We need to understand that our relationship with Christ is far more than to simply know about Him—we need to *be in Him* and He in us.

I hope you can *think* through these verses and see that we are to consider and think of *whatever* is a part of our being, those things added to our souls on this earth (the things we have prided ourselves in perfecting and glorifying), as not having rule and authority over us any longer; and to see instead, that we have gained and been clothed with Christ. We are to use His gift of Himself according to His will and for His glory. We recognize we have a new leader within our core being, our heart, our soul, the One who goes before. I ask you to think on these *things* and so many more, that your nothing might not be wasted now or in eternity.

Ephesians 1 and 2

Previously, we had some fun discussing finding Nemo, but the "nobody matter" is quite serious because nobody matters! I ask you to look at the first two chapters of Ephesians to see how many times "in Him" is used (both in a singular sense for each of us and in the plural sense of being part of the whole body). Again, see the corollary thoughts of our once being nobodies and then becoming somebodies *in Him* (Ephesians 2:19–22), as a part of the body of Christ, "a holy temple in the Lord" and "a dwelling place for God by the Spirit." If you are a Christian, your nothing was chosen "before the foundation of the world" (Ephesians 1:4) to become an adopted something of God as He "works *all things* according to the counsel of His will" (Ephesians 1:11, italics added).

Colossians 1:12-20

This is another passage to ponder and study where Paul first gives "thanks to the Father, who has qualified you to share in the inheritance of the saints in light. He has delivered us from the domain of darkness and transferred us to the kingdom of His beloved Son, in whom we have redemption, the forgiveness of sins"

(Colossians 1:12–14). Then we are taught more truths about Christ—that He created even the things that we do not see or understand, the *no things* to us. So, as you read the remainder of these verses, see how the word *things* is used:

He is the image of the invisible God, the firstborn of all creation. For by Him *all things* were created, in heaven and on earth, visible and invisible, whether thrones or dominions or rulers or authorities—*all things* were created through Him and for Him. And He is before *all things*, and in Him *all things* hold together. And He is the head of the body, the church. He is the beginning, the firstborn from the dead, that *in everything* He might be preeminent. For in Him, all the fullness of God was pleased to dwell, and through Him to reconcile to Himself *all things*, whether on earth or in heaven, making peace by the blood of his cross.

2 Thessalonians 2:8

I have not touched upon many other instances in Scripture where the word *nothing* is used, some because they have a different meaning or context. For instance, in this verse we see that Satan is referred to as the lawless one who will be brought to nothing by the appearance of Christ's coming. In this case, we know that the word *nothing* means that he has and will have no influence or activity, but he will not be absent or entirely gone. He will still have a being and will be eternally separated from each of us as Christians but still under the wrath of God.

The word *nothing* can also mean "not anything except" or "only." We often say this as "nothing but," and the word *only* is a substitute, as in the song with the lyrics, "Nothing but the blood of Jesus."

Matthew 5:3

In the New Testament only a few Greek words are translated as "poor." One means to be needy and poor and is the usual sense of which we think. But the one used in some verses means to be devoid of all things, destitute, to be nothing. It can be used to refer to someone who has none of this world's goods and then means "begging, or destitute of wealth, influence, and position, or helpless, or powerless to accomplish a goal or desire." So, let's look at how the word is used a little differently in the verse from the Sermon on the Mount, the words of Jesus, where the first of the Beatitudes says, "Blessed (or happy) are the *poor* in spirit, for theirs is the kingdom of God." The word *poor* here is used in regard to a person's spirit and has the meaning of being aware of a more inward and conscious spiritual need and, thus, realizing we are truly devoid of everything except what God provides. Thayer's lexicon says such persons who are poor in spirit "most readily give themselves up to Christ's teaching and prove themselves fitted to lay hold of the heavenly treasure." We are indeed poor or "nothing" before the Lord and have need for everything. We do not have breath, water, a bite to eat, or indeed anything except from the Lord. Think of our minds and abilities to read this book, or even being able to think! God has given all we need so that we, beyond ourselves, can give and serve during our entire earthly God-given time, using our very being and abilities. And that giving and serving is not for our benefit or good but for God's glory.

What a verse to meditate and study upon, containing only one of the alternate words in Scripture to help convey the meaning of *nothing* to us! To me it is saying our very spirit, our core being, is happy, satisfied, and blessed when we realize our soul is poor (in the sense of its nothingness), devoid of anything else except the spirit or soul. We realize in our very core the everything that we have added to us while on this earth is from God. We see clearly and know certainly that our state as nothing (soul or spirit only) as it leaves this earth will immediately be present in the kingdom of God (heaven) where one day we will be reunited with our new resurrection body and dwell eternally with Him. Praise the Lord that we know and have the certain hope that our stripped or poor spirit, void of all earthly possessions (time, treasure, talent, body), will be clothed in righteousness with His possession (note the possessive word *theirs* in Matthew 5:3!), which is the kingdom. It is an already-promised-and-done deal as the word *is* teaches us. It is not past as in before we were made beings, or were made poor in spirit, and is not future even though it will take place in our future. Sometimes this is referred to as "already but not yet."

You may want to look up the words to the song "Nothing Without You" by Bebo Norman, as it speaks about the use of various parts of our body in the context of being nothing without the Lord.

Romans 5:5

Here is another concept and verse: "and hope does not put us to shame, because God's love has been poured into our hearts through the Holy Spirit who has been given to us." Romans 5:5 teaches us that love has been poured into our empty hearts when the Holy Spirit changes our hearts to accept Jesus Christ as Savior and Lord. Some have made the metaphor that we have a cross-shaped hole in our hearts that is filled with Christ, who is God's love gift to each person whom He saves.

We often express our love with the phrase, "I love you from the bottom of my heart!" What do we mean by *bottom*? It conveys that our love is completely given to the very last amount—it is gone. Nothing is left; all of our love is expressed—but, actually, there is still a heart and there is still love present. Our heart is "emptied," but it is not empty! It has been emptied of love but still has love. It is reduced as in the phrase "no love left," but we really know that is not true; there is still something beyond the "no love left" because we know there is still love "beneath" and beyond the "bottom." See Ruth 1:21 where Naomi thought she was empty, but indeed she was not!

My wife, Gini, in a drawing phase drew a picture of a cross that seemed to be on its side. I asked her about it as she continued to draw. She told me, "It is a cross on its side, like it would be if it fell to the ground, and you know we are not told and don't know what happened to the cross." She then proceeded to draw another cross shape, and I asked about that. She said,

"I wrote it just above, 'hole of cross.'" I looked, and she had written those words. There was an empty cross, a hole in a cross shape, and her words. I began to think, *YES! there is a "cross-shaped hole" in our empty hearts that Christ fills.*

While on this subject of empty, consider that we often talk about emptying the contents of a package or can. We know that when it is emptied it is still a can, not entirely empty but has something remaining—even if it is minimal or only full of air. The Bible has another word that is used for the concept of empty, poor, or nothing—that word is *poverty*. This word, too, is worth your study and contemplation in its use for seeming nothingness in our impoverished state.

Not Color Is Color?

We have discussed the concept of nothing being something and also that "not anything" is also something, but let's now consider what we think of as *not color* is really color! We have all seen old black and white movies or TV shows and then seen the "colorized" remakes. Are the colors in the remakes true, and if so, how is it done and how is it possible to know what the color was because they were not taken with a color camera? For starters, there is no known color information in true black and white film, but the hues and grays can certainly provide the different shades within the blues of the sky and the greens of the trees. And, once a color is established, computer technology allows continuous finding and assigning of that particular color with its shading to all future locations of that particular type of gray. So, not only is the sky the various shades of blue, and the transition to the various shades of green of trees and grass assigned no matter how the scene moves, but once assigned, the flesh tones and color of clothes can also be automatically determined within what used to be seen as only varying grays.

In addition, there were television shows that were color broadcasts and then recorded from black and white television sets. These televisions could not process or project the color in any way, but old black and white VHS tapes recorded from those black and white only TV sets have recently been examined with complex computer programs and the true colors can be recovered. This is a good example of something that we perceive and actually believe to be absent, or devoid of some aspect or quality, that turns out to have been present all along—in this case, color. The Lord has given us eyes and brains to perceive the color spectrum, so we don't live in a black and white world! We know there are shades of gray within the black, and we all learned in school that true black is a combination of all the colors. But, what we did not learn, because our eyes could not perceive, was that color was present all along in the shows that were broadcast to a black and white TV set! Changes in technology allowed processing of the signals to reveal what the original color was at the time the pictures were taken. While this seemed so amazing at first, we now take it for granted. And, now we know there was actually something called color within what we formerly thought was devoid of color.

Now, let me mess with your mind to cause you to think more! I just wrote that we consider black to be the combination of all colors, and if one color is missing, we do not have true black. So, is black a color? No, because if it is, then one would need to mix that black with all the colors to make black. Only by common definition then is black considered a color. Pure white is the absence of all colors but is also considered a color. Yet another example of something that *is* and we understand in a certain way; however, we do not have a complete understanding. White is the "nothing" of color but is truly something.

Let's go down this rabbit trail just a little further. The true color of something is not what we see because we only see the reflected light that is not part of what is absorbed. So, technically we see pure white because all colors are being reflected and no colors of the light spectrum are absorbed. Again, a white object is the "nothing" of color.

We said that black is really not a color, and because it is the absorption of all colors within the light presented to it, we perceive black only because no light reaches our eye. We see color then only when there is light to be reflected. Therefore, at night in the absence or near absence of light, less and less light is reflected, thus it is harder or impossible to see colors. This is also perceived as black to our eyes.

A Little about Races

At the start of a horse race or a track meet race (when the horses are in the gate or the runners in their blocks), there is complete silence and not anything is being said; no one is moving, some are even holding their breath, and there seems to be a pause in time. But, we know that time is continuing, and while many would say this pause is considered a time of nothing, we term it *silence* yet know that it is still something. Then, the shot is sounded and the race begins.

More about Shadows

Let us explore shadows a bit more as well. When we see a shadow, there has to be a light source and a real something to cast the shadow. While we usually consider a shadow to be nothing, it is really an area of decreased light compared to surrounding areas and can be defined and described by position, shape, and direction. It gives us an idea of whatever has cast the shadow as well as how and where to find that source. But, as I have already hinted, think a moment. Not only is the shadow actually something, but whatever has cast the shadow is only the secondary source of the shadow, as the light is the real source! Many of the shadow examples in the Bible are a literary device to point us back to the source—and ultimately to the True Source, the Light of the world! The shadow is not the real thing, but it does give us enough information to suggest or confirm the real, and the direction to the light. When light comes into a completely dark room, the darkness is dissipated and the room and any objects within are defined. Even though we only see objects and shadows, we know there is light present and the direction from which that light comes! We are to be secondary light sources, reflecting the true Light, helping to cast shadows (and thus provide direction and understanding) within the dark, unsaved world we live in. (See Matthew 5:14–16. Also see Psalm 23:4; Matthew 4:16; Colossians 2:17; Hebrews 10:1; and James 1:17.)

Concerning shadows and nothing, here is part of a very interesting paragraph in section 2.3 of the *Stanford Encyclopedia of Philosophy*:

Indeed, as the only true substance and only true cause, created beings are no more than God's "shadows" or "images." (While "particular minds" deliberate and choose, and so possess a kind of agency, they lack real power and are thus no more than images of divine agency. Because they lack not only power but also consciousness and will, bodies are even further removed from real agency and hence are, as Edwards says, mere shadows of being.) As the only true substance and only true cause, God is the "head" of the system of beings, its "chief part," an absolute sovereign whose power and perfection are so great that "all other beings are as nothing to him, and all other excellency . . . as nothing and less than nothing, . . . in comparison of his."

— Jonathan Edwards
End of Creation, 1765

Is a Wheel Spinning at Its Center?

A spinning wheel intrigues me in that the closer I get to the exact center, I realize that the opposite sides of the wheel are going in opposite directions to allow the back of the wheel to come forward to be utilized again! But, what about the exact center, where there is no spinning movement whatsoever! When I look at a point near the outer edge of the wheel, I realize that point has to travel more distance than points closer to the center, and thus the outer part of the wheel is revolving at a faster speed. Let's use the example of a marching band on a field where they simulate two opposite spokes on a wheel, and we see that there is no center person (because he would not move), while the lines out are facing opposite directions. The innermost person is relaxed as he almost steps in place, while the outermost person is taking giant steps just to keep the line straight!

Although there really is nothing new under the sun, at the same time, we are truly "nothing new" under the Son!

Isometric Exercises

Isometric exercises occur when you use opposing forces of your muscles to push or pull against one another without movement. An example is clasping your hands together and then pushing each hand toward the other with equal force. There is no movement, and it seems that nothing is happening. In reality, however, the exercises do have purpose, and the end result of repeated cycles is added strength and endurance of your muscles. And you certainly get tired when you perform them!

More about Sand

Let us go back to sand castles with a little different twist. When our self-made, carefully built, nearly perfect, and treasured sand castle is constructed where it will be washed away by the next incoming tide, that sand castle will be destroyed. When the Lord changes our hearts, we say His blood washes away and destroys our dead, self-changed, and self-made treasure. We are truly changed, and we realize that our nakedness, our nothing, our soul is what is left. Then our nothing boasts (or glories) in our true Treasure, which is Christ only (see 1 Corinthians 1:27–31). Christ then is our hope of glory and uses His treasure within and through us (see Colossians 1:27).

Consider also my footprints in the sand on the beach that soon fade with wind and surf, but their imprint surely was made and existed. I even know where those of last year were, but I cannot see them. So it is with the imprint of a life lived on earth. Though fading and seeming to disappear with death, the influenced imprint remains in so many ways. Although we might not see anything, the seeming nothing is truly something!

As we come to the end of this book, you might be thinking, *Gene, you wrote things that sometimes seem a bit "off the wall." Granted, you did make me think, but is there anything else beyond nothing?* My answer is simple: although there really is nothing new under the sun, at the same time, we are truly "nothing new" under the Son! There is much more I have in my mind that I did not include. Many others have written about most of it, and the Bible is full of corollary and compelling passages. What I have discussed is the concept of this additional meaning of nothing beyond that traditionally used in our world, along with its use in the Bible passages and some application to our lives. I want to look at two additional separate applications that correlate and complement.

Hebrews 10:34—11:3

The first addition is at the end of Hebrews 10 and the facts presented in chapter 11 concerning faith. In chapter 10, we learn that Christ sacrificed for us, once for all; and then as believers we know that we will be tested and will suffer loss, but joyfully accept the loss:

> since you knew that you yourselves had a better possession and an abiding one. Therefore do not throw away your confidence, which has a great reward. For you have need of endurance, so that when you have done the will of God you may receive what is promised. For, "Yet a little while, and the coming one will come and will not delay; but my righteous one shall live by faith, and if he shrinks back, my soul has no pleasure in him." But we are not of those who shrink back and are destroyed, rather of those who have faith and preserve their souls. Now faith is the assurance of things hoped for, the conviction of things not seen. For by it the people of old received their commendation. By faith we understand that the universe was created by the word of God, so that what is seen was not made out of things that are visible.

We clearly see that faith is not a leap into the unknown but instead is the full assurance and the hope in things to come and promised, based on the truth in the written Word of God. At our deepest and most basic soul level, within our heart, we understand what faith is. We know that we are aliens and strangers on this earth for a season of life, and that with death all the worldly possessions are removed, and yet we have the full assurance of our dwelling with our heavenly Father eternally, praising Him with a new body and clothed in the righteousness of Christ.

2 Corinthians 5

A second application passage is the entire fifth chapter of 2 Corinthians:

> For we know that if the tent that is our earthly home is destroyed, we have a building from God, a house not made with hands, eternal in the heavens. For in this tent we groan, longing to put on our heavenly dwelling, if indeed by putting it on we may not be found naked. For while we are still in this tent, we groan, being burdened—not that we would be unclothed, but that we would be further clothed, so that what is mortal may be swallowed up by life. He who has prepared us for this very thing is God, who has given us the Spirit as a guarantee.
>
> So we are always of good courage. We know that while we are at home in the body we are away from the Lord, for we walk by faith, not

by sight. Yes, we are of good courage, and we would rather be away from the body and at home with the Lord. So whether we are at home or away, we make it our aim to please Him. For we must all appear before the judgment seat of Christ, so that each one may receive what is due for what he has done in the body, whether good or evil.

Therefore, knowing the fear of the Lord, we persuade others. But what we are is known to God, and I hope it is known also to your conscience. We are not commending ourselves to you again but giving you cause to boast about us, so that you may be able to answer those who boast about outward appearance and not about what is in the heart. For if we are beside ourselves, it is for God; if we are in our right mind, it is for you. For the love of Christ controls us, because we have concluded this: that one has died for all, therefore all have died; and He died for all, that those who live might no longer live for themselves but for Him who for their sake died and was raised.

From now on, therefore, we regard no one according to the flesh. Even though we once regarded Christ according to the flesh, we regard him thus no longer. Therefore, if anyone is in Christ, he is a new creation. The old has passed away; behold, the new has come. All this is from God, who through Christ reconciled us to himself and gave us the ministry of reconciliation; that is, in Christ God was reconciling the world to himself, not counting their trespasses against them, and entrusting to us the message of reconciliation. Therefore, we are ambassadors for Christ, God making his appeal through us. We implore you on behalf of Christ, be reconciled to God. For our sake he made him to be sin who knew no sin, so that in him we might become the righteousness of God.

This passage is pretty straightforward in confirming to us the guarantee that each Christian will dwell in heaven forever with our Savior, Lord, and Treasure—as well as an admonishment to not waste our life on earth but to walk and serve in faith. When we leave this world, not only is our old self and our sin taken away—and we will be unclothed of the worldly (mortal) in us—but we will be left with our soul in the presence of God, and then we will have our new resurrected body when Christ returns. This passage is also a mandate to be His ambassador to shine forth His light to a dark world while we are dwelling here, carrying out His purpose for our lives!

Put God First!

I cannot, and this book cannot, teach a bunch of nobodies or no ones to become somebodies or some ones—only God has made your no one into the someone you are, and God is the One who changes hearts. When God changes you, your self-serving someone becomes a different someone, as the Lord gives you the ability and desire to acknowledge Him as Savior and Lord. You then desire to put Him first in all things.

What will you do with what God has given you? This question is pretty well answered by deciding which things in life are first and which things are second. God is the only thing to put first, and all other things are second. C. S. Lewis further clarified this: "Put first things first and we get second things thrown in: put second things first and we lose both first and second things." With my emphasis added, read and see what is written in Ephesians 1:17–23.

> that the God of our Lord Jesus Christ, the Father of glory, may give you a spirit of wisdom and of revelation in the knowledge of Him, having the *eyes of your hearts enlightened*, that you may know what is the hope to which He has called you, what are the riches of His glorious inheritance in the saints, and what is the immeasurable greatness of His power toward us who believe, according to the working of His great might that He worked in Christ when He raised Him from the dead and seated Him at His right hand in the heavenly places, far above all rule and authority and power and dominion, and above every name that is named, not only in this age but also in the one to come. And He put all things under His feet and gave Him as *head over all things* to the church, which is His body, the fullness of *Him who fills all in all.*

"Lord, I Give You My Heart" is a song by Reuben Morgan with beautiful lyrics that I want you to look up on the Internet. (I am sorry I don't have permission to print it here.) The words speak about living our lives so as to finish well by honoring, worshipping, praising, and adoring the Lord with all our heart—and then giving our heart and soul to the Lord to let Him lead and direct our every step for every moment He gives us on this earth.

Ask God to open your eyes (the eyes of your heart, your very core being) to see the *things* that God has given you and properly use them for His glory while you are on this earth. Do not waste your filled-up nothing!

About the Author

Dr. Gene Baillie grew up in rural Nebraska, the oldest of six children and the first member of his family to attend college. He and Gini were married during his first year of medical school. Pathology training and two years of public health service came after medical school, and Gene practiced pathology for thirty-five years in Anderson, South Carolina.

For many years, he taught technologist and pathology courses at a national level, and he was elected to the board of the American Society for Clinical Pathology, serving as their president in 2002–3. He has written several medical articles, including one with his daughter Becky about biblical leprosy.

Gene and Gini raised three biological children—Becky, Kim, and Heather—who are now married and blessed Gene and Gini with eight grandchildren. The Baillies also raised four foster sons who were part of a family of eight children. All eight children are considered part of the Baillie family, as are their children.

The Baillie family also includes many spiritual children and grandchildren as well. Gene and Gini were blessed to travel on mission trips to Korea, Taiwan, Japan, Jamaica, Republic of Congo, and Liberia. They also were a part of planting four churches, including one in Australia, where Gene worked for five years teaching pathology to medical doctors.

He is an elder in the Presbyterian Church in America. Over the years, the Baillie home served as a site for newly started churches and as a place for Gene and Gini to teach inductive Bible studies. For more than a quarter of a century, Gene has been passionate about reading the Bible through each year, and he has encouraged many others, by weekly accountability, to do the same.

Dr. Baillie also wrote *The Journey Home*, a book about walking through and rising above trials of hardship and pain that the Lord allows in our lives. As Gene and Gini saw the Lord provide for them, may we all continue to seek the Lord as the "I AM" who is all sufficient for our every need. This book is also a love story of more than fifty years of marriage and devotion to one another. Go to www.ReadTheJourneyHome.com to order or watch the video on marriage vows.

If you desire to contact the author,
please email GeneBaillie@gmail.com.
Additional copies of the book,
including e-format, can be ordered from
www.ReadNothingMatters.com
or www.ReadGoodBooks.org.

CPSIA information can be obtained at www.ICGtesting.com
Printed in the USA
LVOW07s0406230815

451176LV00001B/1/P